Seven ...
Seven to Follow

By the same author:

Seven to Flee
Seven to Follow

by

RICHARD HOLLOWAY
Bishop of Edinburgh

MOWBRAY
LONDON & OXFORD

Copyright © Richard Holloway 1986

ISBN 0 264 67082 5

First Published 1986
by A. R. Mowbray & Co. Ltd,
Saint Thomas House, Becket Street,
Oxford, OX1 1SJ

Typeset by Cotswold Typesetting Ltd, Cheltenham.
Printed in Great Britain by Cox and Wyman Ltd.,
Reading

British Library Cataloguing in Publication Data

Holloway, Richard
    Seven to flee, seven to follow. –
    (Mowbray's popular christian paperbacks)
    1. Spiritual life   2. Good and evil
    I. Title
    248.4   BV4501.2

    ISBN 0-264-67082-5

FOR MY SEVEN GODSONS
RICHARD
DEREK
RICHARD
THOMAS
LUKE
JONAH
NICHOLAS

CONTENTS

ACKNOWLEDGEMENTS

The author and publisher wish to thank the following for their kind permission to use quotations:

Martin Secker & Warburg Ltd, for a short extract from *Humboldt's Gift* by Saul Bellow.

Executors of the James Joyce Estate, for an extract from *A Portrait of the artist as a young man,* by James Joyce, Jonathan Cape.

Oxford University Press, for an extract from *Faith and Reason* by Richard Swinburne (1981).

John Murray Publishers Ltd, for extracts from Letters Vol. 5, by Hart-Davis and from 'A Lincolnshire Church' and 'Meditation on the A30', both in *Collected Poems* by John Betjeman.

Macmillan Publishers Ltd, for a short extract from *Hugh Walpole: A Biography* by Rupert Hart-Davis (1952).

PREFACE

When Christians are baptised they promise three things: to renounce what is evil, to believe what is true, and to follow what is good. The Revised Catechism answers the question about what was promised on our behalf at Baptism in these words: 'At my Baptism my godparents made three promises to God for me: first, that I would renounce the devil and fight against evil; secondly, that I would hold fast the Christian Faith and put my whole trust in Christ as Lord and Saviour; thirdly, that I would obediently keep God's holy will and commandments and serve him faithfully all the days of my life'. The content of the Christian life is derived from these promises and the struggle to be faithful to them is called Formation by the students of the spiritual life. Christians are embarked on a quest for spiritual maturity that will involve flight from evil, a deepening awareness of the truth and the struggle to achieve goodness. In this programme for living we are, of course, aided and guided by the Holy Spirit, if we will place ourselves under its direction. This book is about two elements in the quest for Christian maturity: the struggle to renounce what is evil and the more important struggle to follow what is good. Evil is summarised in the tradition of sin as sevenfold; and the gifts that come from the Holy Spirit to balance and subdue evil are sevenfold, as well. This book is about the seven deadly sins and the seven gifts of the Holy Spirit.

Sacred or significant numbers probably do not mean much to men and women today, but they once had powerful meaning of an almost mystical sort. There is no absolute reason why anything should be divided into seven or seventeen, but the urge to order and arrange has a strong logic behind it: it helps us to remember the scope, sweep and complexity of the subject under discussion. Sin can be infinitely subdivided in its ramifications, but it helps in self-examination and self-understanding if it is summarised in a manageable way, the sevenfold list does that concisely. The gifts of the Holy Spirit are first mentioned in Isaiah 11.2: 'And the Spirit of the Lord shall rest upon him, the spirit of wisdom and understanding, the spirit of counsel and might, the spirit of knowledge and the fear of the Lord'. It will be obvious that this is a list of six gifts. St. Jerome's translation of the Bible, known as the Vulgate, seems to be the source of the seventh gift, where it is added as 'piety' between knowledge and fear: *spiritus scientiae et pietatis et replebit eum spiritus timoris Domini.* It is in this form that the tradition of the sevenfold dower of the Holy Spirit enters the Christian tradition and it is celebrated in many of our hymns for Pentecost.

> Come, Holy Ghost, our souls inspire,
> And lighten with celestial fire;
> Thou the anointing Spirit art,
> Who dost thy sevenfold gifts impart.

The Golden Sequence is probably the best-loved Whitsun hymn; its last verse says:

> Fill thy Faithful, who confide
> In thy power to guard and guide,
> With thy sevenfold Mystery.

Discerning readers will notice that I have dealt with the seven gifts in reverse order, beginning with Fear of the Lord and ending with Wisdom. If the fear of the Lord is the beginning of Wisdom, as Proverbs informs us, then it seems appropriate to begin at the beginning of our quest for Christian Wisdom, by starting with Fear of the Lord. This gives us the order: Fear, Piety, Knowledge, Courage, Counsel, Understanding and Wisdom; and that is the order in which I discuss them.

RICHARD HOLLOWAY

PART ONE

The Seven Deadly Sins

PRIDE

Crime and punishment, law and order are controversial issues in our society today. The general perception seems to be that there has been an increase in crime and lawlessness and that one of the reasons for this is a breakdown in discipline. Behind the breakdown in discipline, it is sometimes alleged, lies a failure of nerve among influential sections of society who see criminal behaviour as the consequence of social deprivation and not the result of unique human wickedness. For instance, social workers are often said to be 'soft' on crime because they try to discover the reasons behind the bad behaviour of their clients, providing judges and magistrates with background reports and case histories most of which, it is assumed, are designed to diminish the offender's responsibility for the crime in question. According to this point of view, bad behaviour is really the expression of good purposes and desires that have been frustrated and thwarted by the lack of appropriate outlets for self-development and the absence of opportunities that might engage the offender's energies and increase his self-esteem. According to this view, it is not enough to discover criminals and punish them; we must also try to understand the circumstances that contribute to their hatred of society and help them to find legitimate outlets for their frustrated ambitions and unfulfilled needs. As is usual in these affairs, there are two sides to the question, though protagonists in the debate tend to ignore the facts on the other side. Human irrationality and wickedness, as well as low intelligence and lack of affection from one's parents, can all contribute something to the emergence of criminal behaviour. And it is fairly obvious that there is a strong correlation between poverty and crime, though it is probably not precise enough to talk of causes here. Apart from that innate tendency to wickedness which is in all of us and which must be controlled, there are other factors that undoubtedly contribute to bad behaviour and understanding them will help us to understand some of the roots of crime.

This is not an essay on crime, but it may be that what is a legitimate approach towards understanding criminals a little better may also have something to teach us about the sins that flesh is heir to. If we apply some of the insights of social work theory to sin itself we might get some interesting and possibly helpful results. If we adopt this approach we will see at once that there is a real parallel. If we ask what sin is, or what wickedness is, it is difficult not to answer in negatives: a bad person is someone in whom there is little or no goodness. When we look at it closely, wickedness is itself a kind of deprivation, something that has only a negative existence, something that could not exist at all if goodness did not exist first, since it is the negation of goodness. Evil is the negation of good. An example might help us to understand this. The sin of gluttony seems positive enough when we first think about it; it is inordinate consumption, overindulgence. But how do we know what 'too much' is in this context? Only because there is a sort of normal standard from which gluttony has declined, a proper or normal amount to eat: anything over that is a departure from the norm, a falling-away from the standard. So a glutton is someone who has failed to find the right balance in satisfying genuine human needs. And all sin seems to have something of this character. It is wrongly directed effort; it is a good drive that fails to find the right object; or it is something good in itself that is done to excess. This will become clearer later in the book, but something of what we are trying to express is suggested by one of the words in the New Testament for our English verb 'to sin'. The word that is used most often for sin is an archery term that means 'to miss the mark'. We have a picture of someone who is aiming at the bull's eye on the target, but for some reason, personal or circumstantial, he misses the mark and the arrow goes elsewhere. All sinful activity seems to have this characteristic: it is really a frustration or misdirection of genuine needs and impulses. A river that is damned or blocked and unable to follow its natural route will overflow its banks and find an alternative way. Our life is something like that. It is meant to flow in a certain direction; it is like a great force of energy, constantly on the move. If it does not find the right direction, the appropriate outlet, the real target, it will find alternatives because it must go somewhere, do something with its life-force. All sin is largely misdirected effort, energy that has not found creative outlets. It is all a bit like someone stumbling about in the dark, knocking things over and creating absolute chaos in a search for that elusive light switch.

Now, if there is some truth in this, we have a more helpful way of dealing with the sins that beset us. If we really investigate them and ask for a background report on them in the same way that the judge will ask the social worker, then we might find out what we are really looking for when we fall into sin and try, in future, to go in the right direction. In other words, let us find a way of understanding and rehabilitating sin. Let us find out what sin is really looking for. Let us stop hammering away at sin, placing it in the dock with bowed head while our denunciations flow off its back. We know it will only crawl away and do the same thing all over again. Let us, instead, invite sin in for a private discussion over hot tea and ginger biscuits. Let us try some positive reinforcement, a bit of praise. Let us praise the seven deadly sins or, at the very least, try to understand them.

The old teachers, with their interesting passion for classification according to significant numbers, divided sin into seven main groups, though they are all related. Here, then, are the magnificent seven: Pride, Envy, Covetousness, Anger, Gluttony, Lust and Sloth. It seems a pity that there is no well-known verse or mnemonic to help us remember the list, of the 'every good boy deserves favour' variety, though there is no reason at all why we should not create our own. Most of the obvious combinations of letters make them sound like government quangos, such as SLAGPEC or GLAPECS. Readers might like to spend a few innocent minutes developing their own mnemonics. This writer offers one feeble example: Some Lazy Authors Give Publishers Extra Chores!

Pride, of course, is the grandfather of all the sins; it is the root sin, the basic disposition behind every wrong or misdirected effort. Pride has been defined negatively as the primal disobedience, the act that got the whole sorry enterprise of human sinfulness going. How does it arise and, remembering what we have just discussed, how did whatever it is get misdirected in the first place, and where should it have been going? One possible way to answer that series of questions is by observing that there is in human beings what we might call a force towards worship, a profound need to identify value and esteem or adore it. There is in all of us a powerful need to give ourselves totally to some person or good, some cause or great enterprise. This need in us is like a mighty river pulling and rushing with an almost gravitational intensity towards the sea. Spiritual writers would say that the real goal of all that undifferentiated effort and striving is God, who acts upon us the way the moon acts upon the sea, causing great tides of longing and home-sickness that ebb and flow in our hearts and minds. God is the great and tranquil sea we long to pour ourselves into, but, for ancient and mysterious reasons, we constantly frustrate and divert the strong flow of our life's direction. It eddies and surges in all directions, seeking outlets, carving channels, all designed to carry the force of our longing towards some object that will fulfil it.

Pride is the vain effort to make ourselves the goal and destination of our own lives' longing, so all this energy for worship, this search for the good object, becomes turned in upon ourselves and we become the object of our own adoration. Pride, therefore, is the placing of the self in the space that only God can properly occupy. Pride is, quite precisely, to be self-centred; to see ourselves as the centre of all significance and value; to make ourselves the measure of all good. Our first and abiding temptation is to be as God, and humanity's history is the record of that misdirected longing. Pride is self-esteem raised to an inordinate level, so that all sense of proportion is lost, not only between ourselves and God, but also between ourselves and other people, who are themselves struggling against the same pathological condition. Pride is the great obstacle that stands in the way of an honest relationship with God, but it also lies at the root of all human conflict. It is pride that fuels all those interminable hostilities that disfigure human history and it is pride that inhibits reconciliation between disputants long after the events that occasioned the conflict have receded into the past.

How are we to approach this sin? How can we understand it, attempt to re-habilitate it, find it a rightful outlet? We must first recognize that we have this need to worship within ourselves, this need to value and give worth to something. And part of this need to give worth and value to something must be focused on ourselves. It is essential for us to have a genuine sense of our own worth and value, to have a proper sense of our own dignity. God has given us real value and importance, and if it is taken from us or denied to us it will thwart and frustrate a genuine drive in our nature. It is well-known that many aggressive and over-bearing people are fighting against a sense of their own inadequacy. A lot of human pride has this kind of insecurity at its roots. An obvious example of this kind of fear-mechanism is the racial pride of white South Africans. This is due, at least in part, to a fear of being overwhelmed and rendered racially insignificant by their more numerous black fellow countrymen. Most racial pride is rooted in fear and ignorance. Pride is a distortion of a genuine need. We must have a real sense of our own worth, but that worth is never absolute and it is always vulnerable to the actions of others. More profoundly, we must search for those avenues of transcendence that will take us away from the maze of dead ends that constitute the solitary self. The search for value and worth is a corporate enterprise, involving the whole human family. Part of that perennial search obviously lies in seeking a right relationship with God who is the only absolute good, but an equally important part must lie in the quest for the common good. All the forms of pride; private, racial, group and national, are vain efforts to place the part above the whole, and they do violence to obvious human realities. But the parts have a role, and if individuals, families, tribes and races are not afforded legitimate outlets for their own need for self-esteem then stress and distortion occur, and we get all the frightful symptoms of human pride: touchiness, resentment, acute sensitivity, violent reaction to criticism, conceit, arrogance, violence, all the way up to racial or group domination and unscrupulous control over the lives of others.

Tackling this sin on the collective level is the permanent duty of diplomats and peace makers. They are called upon to pick their way through the intricacies of human rivalries and conflicts as they seek to establish the rights of minorities to have their share of the good things of life. It is a task that calls for endless patience and a profound sympathy for the way human beings continue to get in their own way.

How do we tackle this sin in ourselves? We can put the answer in one word: humour. A sense of humour about ourselves is the main antidote to personal pride. If we can laugh at ourselves it means that we see ourselves in proportion; we refuse to take ourselves too seriously; we see the incongruity between our public posturing and the reality of what we are in private. The next time we are tempted to think more highly of ourselves than we ought to think, or to behave in a high-handed or contemptuous way, we should stop and think about what we are really like. We should ask ourselves why we are behaving in this way; we should find out what force is really pushing us; we should try to discover the secret third party in the dispute, our own private agenda of hurt or self-contempt that constantly complicates our relationships with others. Above all we must learn not to take ourselves too seriously. After all, there is scarcely a more comical sight in all creation than this naked little biped, homo sapiens, standing there like a toad on a pebble surrounded by a great lake, yet puffed up with his own importance.

ENVY and COVETOUSNESS

Envy and covetousness, or jealousy and avarice as they are sometimes called, are closely related sins. Many people, in fact, confuse them, but there is an important distinction to be made between them. The covetous man wants to possess his neighbour's goods. In the words of the Tenth Commandment, he wants to possess his neighbour's house, or his neighbour's wife, or his neighbour's servant or maid, or his neighbour's ox or ass. So the sin of covetousness is positive: it is a craving, gnawing desire for something you do not possess. Envy, on the other hand, is not a positive sin; it is entirely negative. The envious woman regrets her neighbour's good; she grieves secretly over her neighbour's luck. Envy has been defined as sorrow for another's good. It can also take the form of secret satisfaction at the misfortunes of our friends, what the Germans call *schadenfreude,* which means, literally, 'shame-joy', malicious joy in the misfortunes of others. Let us tackle envy first.

The first thing to note is that envy is a sin among equals. For instance, I am not a scientist, so I am not likely to feel envy for a fifty year old biologist who has just received the Nobel prize for science. However, I am likely to feel envy towards a fellow priest with whom I was at college when he is promoted because of his brilliant preaching and well-known pastoral effectiveness. Envy is a sin among equals. Envy is common among all groups. If we listen to a discussion among any group of colleagues we are bound to detect it from time to time. What are its characteristics?

Envy's most dominant charcteristic is negative: it offers no pleasure, no satisfaction at all. Every other sin offers some gratification at some time or other, but envy is completely without fun. It is an empty and desolating experience from beginning to end. It is the meanest sin in the book, and this is why few people ever confess it publicly. They will admit to being proud or lustful or bad-tempered, but envy is something they keep bottled up, so that it gnaws away inside them like a cancer. One of the maxims of La Rochefoucauld captures this joyless secrecy perfectly: 'We often pride ourselves on even the most criminal passions, but envy is a timid and shame-faced passion we never dare acknowledge'. When envy has taken us over it produces certain other symptoms.

The most conspicuous symptom of envy is malice. Envious folk have a peculiar gift for chipping away at the reputation of others, praising them in one breath and damning them with some qualifying phrase in the next. They are specially adept at noticing the defects of others. We have all heard them in operation: 'John is very charming and he does speak well, don't you think, but he does rather enjoy the limelight, doesn't he, and one can never have a *conversation* with him since he insists on doing all the talking'. 'My dear, you look *wonderful,* so well *preserved*! How do you do it?'

Another characteristic of the envious person is hypocrisy. Envy is a sin among equals, among brothers and sisters, so it strikes in those relations where love is supposed to rule. When we hear of the good fortune of a friend or equal we can speak one thing but feel another. We can express delight, but we have to draw it up from a well of bitterness. These rivalries can occur between families or neighbours, giving rise to a very common situation in which a mother will give a glowing report of the activities of her talented children to her neighbour who, secretly disappointed by her own children's ordinariness, will feign enthusiastic interest. Sometimes the hypocrisy of the envious can be detected in their faces by the discerning eye. There is usually a certain detectable tightness to the smile and the eyes invariably give it away by their inability to relax on demand. We should not, however, be too hard on this type of hypocrisy. It is, as La Rochefoucauld reminded us, the 'homage paid by vice to virtue'. We feel we ought to be pleased at our neighbour's good fortune, so we act the part, and that is probably better than the dishonest honesty that is meant to hurt, of the blunt man who says exactly what he feels. Of course, even this acted virtue is detectable, especially if it is overdone. One of the signs of hidden envy is exaggerated admiration. If we are profuse with our compliments it is probably because we have fallen into the trap of secret sorrow at the excellence of our friend. Real respect for another always has a certain reserve about it, a certain quietness and confidence. Only the unconfident have to send up a barrage of compliments.

Yet another characteristic of envy is dejection. Envy is sorrow for another's good, but it can also produce sorrow over our own lack of good; it can produce dejection. Dejection comes from a Latin word that means 'to throw out or over', and the dejected person feels cast aside, thrown out. It can be very depressing to witness the blessing or popularity of another. A girl can be dejected by the beauty of her sister; a man can be depressed by the charm and brilliance of a colleague. Those who have little can be dejected by those who have too much. Those who feel themselves to be playing out life in one of the minor divisions can be depressed by the blazing good fortune of their erstwhile colleagues who have made it into the big time. And the life of the religious is not miraculously exempted from this experience. Jesus reminded us that a prophet was not usually without honour, 'save in his own country'.

Finally, envy may lead on to covetousness or avarice, the itching hunger for the good things of life, the success and possessions and popularity that others have. And this brings us to the root of both sins. At the root of both envy and covetousness lies a terrible sense of inadequacy and inferiority. Those who are really covetous try to buy off their self-doubts and insecurities with what sociologists call 'status symbols'. They try to remove their inward doubts by surrounding themselves with all the trappings or symbols of success. The proof of this is that the covetous are never really satisfied. The things they buy or covet do not meet their real needs, so their sense of satisfaction quickly fades. They need more and more. Much advertising relies on this fact: it constantly holds out to people the promise of mysterious satisfactions if only they will take the latest model with the real leather. But this never meets our real needs, so we go on wanting more and more and more. Thomas Carlyle captured it perfectly:

Will the whole Finance Ministers and Upholsterers and Confectioners of Modern Europe undertake, in joint company, to make one Shoeblack HAPPY? They cannot accomplish it, above an hour or two: for the Shoeblack also has a Soul quite other than his Stomach; and would require, if you consider it, for his permanent satisfaction and saturation, simply this allotment, no more, and no less: *God's infinite Universe altogether to himself,* therein to enjoy infinitely, and fill every wish as fast as it rose. Oceans of Hochheimer, a Throat like that of Ophiuchus: speak not of them; to the infinite Shoeblack they are as nothing. No sooner is your ocean filled, than he grumbles that it might have been of better vintage. Try him with half of a Universe, of an Omnipotence, he sets to quarrelling with the proprietor of the other half, and declares himself the most maltreated of men. Always there is a black spot in our sunshine: it is even, as I said, the *Shadow of Ourselves.* (*Sartor Resartus,* book 2, chapter ix)

Covetousness can show itself in many ways, and not just in the conspicuous consumption of gadgets and latest models. We can use people in the same way. The compulsive womanizer, for instance, is often more guilty of covetousness than of lust. His power over women is really an elaborate game played out to cover his own anxiety and fear. He may be too afraid to commit himself finally and sacrificially to a real and enduring relationship, so he bales out time after time at the moment of decision, his life littered with the emotional debris of last year's, last week's, or even last night's models. All the so called great lovers were men of this stamp: Casanova, Don Juan and Frank Harris were emotional cripples who hid from the knowledge of their own emptiness behind a lady killer's reputation. There is a certain type of woman who plays the same, sad game. She is often an ageing film star who has to be surrounded by a band of young, adoring males in order to feel that she really exists, and that those lines she detected in this morning's mirror only make her more fascinating. There are, in fact, many men and women who are pathologically afraid to grow old and lose their good looks, because they have built their lives around their ability to attract the opposite sex.

However it presents itself, either in the gnawing and lonely bitterness of envy or in the itching compulsive desires of covetousness, at the bottom of both sins is the same cause: an overwhelming sense of inadequacy and a deep longing to be accepted and appreciated and valued. And we are all in this situation. Our mean old envies and our raddled and pathetic sins of covetousness come from a source that, deep down, is only assuaged by the real object of our longing – Eternity. As Carlyle reminded us, 'the Shoeblack also has a Soul quite other than his Stomach', and we cannot fill the soul with objects appropriate only to the stomach, though we go on trying. The real answer to these two sad little sins is the saving knowledge that we are loved and accepted by God as we are.

God does not have to be, indeed cannot be, impressed by the multitude and magnificence of our achievements, any more than good parents require their children to be brilliant and successful before accepting and loving them. God accepts us as we are, with all our weaknesses and inadequacies. God accepts us, though we may be unacceptable in our own eyes. This is the only really lasting answer to this problem. In the knowledge that we are accepted by God we can gradually learn to relax and accept ourselves. We no longer have to compete against ourselves or against our friends. Accepted by God, we must learn to accept ourselves. When we do that we will realise that when we envy and covet we are trying to fill our souls with shadows, not with substance. What we lack is always close at hand. Our only ultimate need is God, and God has made himself available.

In addition to learning to relax in the knowledge that we are indeed loved and accepted by God, we must capture something of the generosity of God by rejoicing in the gifts of others. It is tragic and preposterously egocentric to interpret the glories and richness of the varieties of human achievement as a threat to our own self-worth. But we have learned that egocentricity, radical self-centredness, is precisely our problem, so the struggle for ungrudging generosity towards others will probably engage us to the end of our lives. It is a struggle that is well expressed in a prayer written in the seventeenth century by Thomas Fuller:

Lord, I perceive my soul deeply guilty of
  envy.
I had rather thy work were undone than
  done better by another than by myself.
Dispossess me, Lord, of this spirit
And turn my envy into holy emulation;
Yes, make other men's gifts to be mine, by
  making me thankful to thee for them.

ANGER

There are several sins that have their roots in our instinctive nature; they are a pathological development of something that is, in itself, good and essential. The sin of anger has its root in an essential instinctive reaction: it is part of a built-in response to danger. It seems to have two phases, what we might call 'display' and 'retaliation'. It is probably best studied in children or animals. Let us look, first of all, at 'display'. Psychologists suggest that when a child or animal is threatened in some way by danger or anxiety a set of physical and emotional reactions come into play which provides the energy necessary for meeting the unknown situation of danger. The display is shown in young children by kicking, stamping, slashing and holding the breath. In animals it is shown by a sort of pantomime act of ferocity, in baring of the teeth, fluffing out of feathers or bushing out the tail. Now, at first this sort of behaviour is not really directed against anyone in particular, but with increasing age the behaviour is directed against the source of danger itself and we move into the phase of retaliation. Instead of standing and screaming or rolling about on the floor, the child starts to punch and bite; it starts fighting.

The roots of all this lie away back in our primitive past. Behaviour like this had a certain amount of survival value: you had to defend yourself if you were to survive. Most of us have these built in responses to external danger, and there are certain people in whom the ability to respond to danger from outside is very highly developed. In primitive society these people would be the best fighters and the natural leaders. We can still see how this works by studying children who are, to a certain extent, a primitive society. Certainly, when I was a boy the best fighters were also the natural leaders. Most of the boys in my school were studied as closely as racing horses by their fans, their form carefully noted. The leaders were those who had a highly developed ability to respond to danger with a swift punch on the nose and a scrupulous disregard for the Queensberry Rules. Anger acted as a sort of energizer or fuel that set the defensive behaviour in movement, a necessary response in more primitive societies, but one that we have carried with us from the forests and caves into modern times.

That was all very well for cave dwellers, we might say, but we do not need it today. That is probably true, but it is still there, though it operates differently. The root of the whole thing seems to lie in our own comfort or safety. We still guard our little selves as carefully as cavemen. Certain outside events disturb or threaten us and they can trigger off a chain reaction of response that we still call anger. There seem to be four types of response, one often leading to the other in a mounting crescendo that can be very frightening.

The first response is impatience. Impatience is the first phase of anger; it switches on the ignition and gets the motor running. How does it operate? It seems to do something like this: here we are inside ourselves, intent upon our own little programme, with our own little timetable, and something happens that interrupts or threatens our private arrangements. It may be a bus that is late or a child who keeps interrupting the delicious flow of our own carefully argued conversation. Whatever it is, it sets up an opposition to our own plans, it disturbs our own intensity, and slowly the engine of defence begins to wind up. We feel a growing physical discomfort, a tightening in the chest, a pulling-in of the face muscles, very much as a caveman must have reacted to the first sniff of danger flowing down-wind. If we can, we act out the impatience. Instead of waiting at the stop for the delayed bus we set out to move to the next one because we can't stand still. Inevitably, of course, the bus glides smugly past us midway between stops, rendering us incoherent with anger. Or we may just tap our feet and mangle our gloves. Whatever we do, impatience is the beginning of a sequence that can lead anywhere.

The next phase is retaliation. In our kind of

society the retaliation is likely to be verbal. Something begins to irritate us; we feel the anger swirling impatiently inside us; something out there is beginning to attack us in some way, giving pain to us; so we lash out. As we might say, we 'bite their heads off'. Another word for this is *sarcasm*, which comes from a Greek word that means to tear the flesh. We suddenly lash out, unleashing the wounding insult, the word that tears the flesh. The retaliation may be physical if we are not very good at finding words, or if we have run out of them. After all, they say that physical violence is the last resort of the verbally incompetent. By this time the situation is escalating, and we are well on the way to phase three, the danger phase.

This is the phase of passion or lack of control. Something finally snaps within us and all proportion and moderation are abandoned; we go over to total attack. This may take the form of verbal passion of an extreme sort: ranting and raving with a red face and staring eyeballs, an outburst of rage that is out of all proportion to the offence that has been committed. People who are in a passion give the impression that they are fighting for their lives, though it may only be over some triviality. Even more frightening is the physical reaction. And here we might think of the mother who has been pushed beyond endurance because she is cooped up in a small flat with four children who make constant and noisy demands upon her, pushing against her patience until something breaks within her and she picks one of them up and beats him with mindless fury, totally lacking in control. This is known as 'the battered baby syndrome', and it is increasingly common in our tense and undisciplined society. Many murders are committed in this state, many relationships destroyed, many marriages permanently damaged, and many fatal road accidents are triggered by the same series of events. It is passion when the anger instinct is allowed to operate freely without control. John Betjeman captured the whole thing in his *Meditation on the A30:*

"You're barmy or plastered, I'll pass you,
    you bastard –
  I *will* overtake you. I *will!*"
As he clenches his pipe, his moment is ripe
  And the corner's accepting its kill.

Then the grimmest and most poisonous phase emerges. After the hostilities are over, the passion is spent, we move into the phase of brooding and resentment, a sort of slow, smouldering anger that turns and turns upon itself, fanning up its resentment, pouring endlessly over the offence that created the situation in the first place. There is even a delicious pain attached to this. We enjoy our sulks the way we enjoy pushing at a loose tooth. We can't leave it alone, so we brood and probe and stir and mope. O, the morbid joy of going into the garden to eat worms! This is the phase of slow death. It can lead to total breakdown in relationships; members of the same family can cease to address a single word to each other; husband and wife can live under the same roof and never exchange a meaningful remark; members of the same congregation can snub each other for years, living out a hideous contradiction of the faith they profess, for a reason they have long since forgotten. This is anger at its final and most malignant phase, seeping through the whole personality.

There can be no doubt that anger deserves its place as a deadly sin. It is a killer spiritually and can be a killer physically, and it lies at the root of much that is wrong with us and our society. The real trouble lies in that caveman who lurks in each of us, nearer the surface in some than in others. Cave dwellers walk through life warily, constantly on the lookout for danger and attack, prepared to shoot first and ask questions later. But life is not really as dangerous as that. Most of the people whose attack we fear are just as apprehensive as we are, and their imagined threats are often really only defences against our own anxious hostility. If we let cave dwellers dictate policy all hell will break loose, and frequently does. What we must try to do is to live outside ourselves, to get out of the little fortress we have built round ourselves and start living towards other people– perhaps by trying to understand why they appear to be threatening us, instead of pulling out our handgun and blasting back at them. The name for this kind of behaviour is love. Love, unlike anger, goes out from the self towards the other. It opens itself out; it does not build defences round itself. It is the open hand, not the clenched fist. Love, the systematic willing of the other person's good, is the only effective antidote to anger. The only other thing we ought to notice is this: when our anger does break out, as break out it will, we must act quickly to minimise the damage. We must, above all, refuse to enter the malignant phase of brooding resentment. As Jesus taught us, we must not let the sun go down on our anger; rather, we must agree with our adversary quickly, while we are in the way with him. And it is worthwhile to remember an ancient Persian aphorism: 'An ill-humoured man is a prisoner at the mercy of an enemy from whom he can never escape'.

LUST and GLUTTONY

Lust and gluttony, though they can have tragic consequences, are by far the most amiable of the seven deadly sins. They are often to be found in kind and attractive people whose humble awareness of their own frailty is disarming and can lead to a kind of tolerant wisdom. By the same token, many of the people who must successfully expunge these sins from their heart end with a personality that can be characterised by a harsh and unlovely strictness. That is why the paradox noted by Joubert rings true: 'Of the two, I prefer those who render vice lovable to those who degrade virtue'. It is also the case that we tend to denounce the vices that are more blatant in their effects, while the more insidious are often ignored by us, and the sins of lust and gluttony are much more easily discerned than some of the others. It is also true that we find it easy to denounce vices that no longer tempt us, following the well-known principle of moral selectivity, whereby vices and virtues are graded in importance according to our subjective response to them. That is why La Rochefoucauld observed that 'when the vices give us up we flatter ourselves that we are giving up them'. The selfrighteousness of the elderly is more often the consequence of inanition than of mortification. We must not romanticise or trivialise the sins of the flesh, but we probably ought to recognize that Christians have too often treated them as though they were the only sins in the book. Lust and gluttony are dangerous, but it is best if we approach them with some tenderness and sensitivity as we seek to understand them.

Central to everything we have been discussing is a single recognition: sin is a good which has somehow become misdirected; it is an element or aspect of life that has been disproportionately inflated. Sin is imbalance or disorder, disharmony or disproportion. Behind it there usually lies a search for balance or order, harmony or proportion, but, being what we are, we never entirely find it. Gluttony and lust are examples of fundamental instincts, good in themselves, that have become disordered. They are, as we have seen, more amiable sins than the sins of the mind and spirit, such as envy and pride, and most moralists hold them to be less culpable because they are so deeply rooted in our instinctual nature. There is something else that ought to be noted. The human spirit and personality is a frail and complicated thing and most of us are formed and programmed to a great extent by causes beyond our control. This is particularly true of our sexual nature, which seems peculiarly vulnerable to pressures and relationships almost unconsciously experienced in our earliest years. I have known one or two men who were in the grip of bizarre sexual deviations for which there was no socially acceptable outlet. I have known people whose whole sexual longing was focused on very young children, for instance. All these people were victims of forces they themselves were unable to control, and their lives were often deeply tragic as a result. In addition to this mysterious propensity for aiming at inappropriate targets, the sexual instinct and the need to feed ourselves can become substitute outlets for other unfulfilled longings. Promiscuity can be caused by a vain search for love or appreciation, and there is a well known connection between over-eating and loneliness. So we do well to remember our Lord's words, 'judge not', and to remember the famous epigram 'to know all is to forgive all'. Only God, of course, knows all the factors that have made us what we are, and he is a merciful judge.

The fact is, however, that most of us have some freedom in these matters. It may not be much, but it can be increased by joyful discipline. At the root of the misuse of those instincts is what philosophers call the hedonistic fallacy. This comes from the Greek word *hedonē*, pleasure. It has been observed that if we pursue pleasure we fail to get it. Pleasure is a by-product of many activities. The problem arises because of a mysterious tendency in our nature: we try to separate the pleasure from the act that gives it and go after it for its own sake. Unfortunately, it does not work for long. In the case of sexual pleasure, let us see what happens. Sexual activity is deeply pleasurable. For Christians it is a sacrament: it is the outward expression and celebration of the love and commitment that two people have for each other. Now, if we try to remove the pleasure of sex from the rich context of a committed relationship and focus our attention on the glandular release that lies at the biological centre of the act, we are not treating either ourselves or the other person as a total person, but as a means to a private pleasure. We are essentially using each other. Of course, we all use each other in many different ways, often in ways worse than sexual exploitation, but it is nevertheless very sad. We call it exploitation, the using of another person for our own pleasure. It may even be with consent: two people can agree to exploit each other. But the end result is always sad and dispiriting and ultimately joyless. The really tragic thing is that the pursuit of pleasure in this way, in and for itself, is the pursuit of a mirage, because pleasure does not exist in its own right; it is a fleeting and elusive thing, spinning off from all sorts of solid activities.

This leads us to the second aspect of this sad state of affairs. Because the pursuit of pleasure for its own sake is always ultimately unsatisfying, we open the way to what is called the addictive cycle. We become dependent on the pleasure, the act of release; we come to need it for its own sake. And this is where it takes its revenge. If our sexual relations with others are not the expression of real, committed love, but simply the pursuit of pleasure, the pleasure soon departs. It is useless to deny that it is present for a time, but it does not wear well unless other things are right. We lose our interest in what the other person's body can offer us, the excitement and the mystery that attracted us in the first place soon leave as we become familiar with the secret that had beset us. It all becomes stale and we move on elsewhere in our pursuit of pleasure, and as it eludes us increasingly we become more and more desperate in our search.

Gluttony has the same characteristics. It is simply the name we give to the pursuit of the pleasure attached to the satisfying of our bodily appetites. The person who drinks too much, or smokes too much is as much a glutton as the person who overeats. We can take it further than that: the person who talks too much, the compulsive prattler who invades our quietness and space with voracious and uninterruptible talk, is as much a glutton as the person who can't stop eating. Lust and gluttony share many characteristics, but their main agreement lies in this: they have lost all balance and proportion. They do not see the natural appetites as instincts that have to be balanced by other considerations; instead, they allow them a disproportionate role, and they can end by dominating and controlling the whole personality. The full tragedy lies in the fact that, at the end, the gluttonous and the lustful are deprived of the pleasures that once ensnared them. The drunkard is driven by a dominating compulsion that lacks all pleasure, and he often ends by seeking oblivion from the torment. This is the irony: pleasure pursued for its own sake becomes torment. If we will not learn to control and direct our own urges, the day may come when they will direct and control us. There is no misery like that misery; the misery of complete powerlessness. This is the real tragedy of these apparently amiable instincts: pursued for their own sake, they can rob us of our freedom.

It is all very depressing, but it is never too late to start again. We are never too old to grow and develop and change, and through all the struggle with our own intractable nature, God still loves and forgives us. There is no quick cure, of course. We have to learn discipline; we have to learn to control the whole personality so that it works, not for its own ends, but towards the real purpose of life, which is the service and enjoyment of God and the love of our neighbour. The old cure is the only one that works: fasting. Fasting has an old-fashioned ring about it, but it was our Lord's way, so it must teach us something today. Fasting is the name we give to the assertion of control by the whole personality over any of its parts; it is the control of our appetites by mind and will. It is a process of training and control through which the reason and will direct the drives of our nature, and not the other way round. If we are truly free, then there ought not to be anything in our lives that we could not deny ourselves, at least for a season, whether it is sex, or food, or drink, or tobacco, or listening to the sound of our own voice. The general label for this kind of balanced restraint is temperance. The temperate person enjoys the good things God has given us, but they are not allowed to dominate or become disproportionately important.

There is one final thing we should note. The outward act of fasting is good for us, in and of itself, but something may be missing: the inward attitude. We can achieve no lasting peace and joy in our lives until they are surrendered to God. Fasting from all our appetites can serve that goal if we offer it to God as a token of our self-offering. Then our fasting can become precious and positive, and not just an act of self-denial: it can become the outward and visible sign of a life made available to God.

SLOTH

One of the most lovely volumes of prayer ever produced is Eric Milner White's *My God My Glory*. It is a book of enormous richness, whose prayers ought to be said slowly and contemplatively, sipped and savoured like a good wine. But even Homer nods on occasion and there is one prayer in the book that gives credence to a widespread heresy. It is the prayer 'Work' and it contains this fateful line: 'So bless our work; thou canst not bless idleness'. It is paradoxical that such a sentiment should be discovered in a book of prayers that was clearly the fruit of years of quiet, spiritual idling as the author ruminated on the glory of God. It is said that Milner White was often seen sitting in a chair in the garden at King's, Cambridge, slowly meditating and transcribing his prayers. Many of the prayers come from other sources, but most of them are the result of the author's own contemplation upon the mysteries of creation and the joys and struggles of the spiritual life, and that contemplation can only have been purchased at the expense of what we would conventionally understand by work.

It might be argued, of course, that he was working when he was praying, but that does not quite meet the issue. It would be possible to define work so broadly that it included all purposive activity, including that leisured reverie that is an important element in various kinds of creative endeavour, but that is to remove most of the distinctiveness from the word. The word 'work' *can* be used in this broad way to describe any activity that is appropriate to the person; it is something that is or was done. If idleness is a necessary element in what has to be done in, say, the crafting of a beautiful prayer, then work can be claimed to include idleness, but this is really a piece of pedantry that is far from the conventional understanding. The conventional difference between work and idleness is, in fact, set out in the prayer in question where God is exhorted to 'bless our work; thou canst not bless idleness'. But why not? Why is idleness displeasing to God or why is it *held* to be displeasing to him?

Part of the answer must clearly come from the story of the Fall of Adam and Eve in The Book of Genesis. As a result of their disobedience God tells Adam:

Because you have listened to the voice of your wife, and have eaten of the tree of which I commanded you, 'You shall not eat of it', cursed is the ground because of you; in toil you shall eat of it all the days of your life; thorns and thistles it shall bring forth to you; and you shall eat the plants of the field. In the sweat of your face you shall eat bread till you return to the ground, for out of it you were taken; you are dust, and to dust you shall return. (3.17-19)

It is undoubtedly a fact that this text is an accurate description of the drudgery to which the poor have been committed for thousands of years, as they struggle to eke out a living from a harsh and unyielding world, but it is surely not necessary to conclude that God has placed the curse of work upon men and women in this world for ever. If we may speak in theological categories for a moment, we could say that because of the Fall of Adam all human activity is somehow vitiated and distorted, but it is the work of Christ to rescue us from these consequences, to redeem us, restore us to an experience of life that is able, in some way, to transcend the consequences of the Fall. The curses of Genesis are not ineluctable laws; they are clear statements of the consequences of certain aspects of our human nature, but we are not bound by the curse of toil any more than women are bound to the pains of childbirth that are also prophesied in this same chapter. Nevertheless, these Old Testament prophecies have had a profound effect on human consciousness and they have gone far to contribute to the development of what is sometimes called 'the Protestant Work Ethic'.

According to that ethic we are here to toil and spin, not enjoy ourselves idly like the lilies of the field who do neither. Thus, there has been bred into a certain type of consciousness a suspicion of creation and the enjoyment it can offer. The natural order, far from being filled with signals of God's presence and reflections of his beauty, is a spiritual minefield for the person of faith. It is littered with temptations and cluttered with vanities. The creation, far from mediating the divine presence is experienced as God's greatest rival and it has to be sternly denied. The only safe relationship with creation is exploitation and domination. We are in the world to work, to tame and control the natural order. The consequences of this dour theology have been enormous. They have led to all the miracles and blessings of modern technology, and they have marked the earth with our curse and smeared and bleared it with our toil. Work is a very mixed blessing, as are all human activities. One of the profound spiritual consequences of the work ethic is the denigration of that necessary leisure which is a vital element in the formation of a healthy and balanced human personality. It is an instructive paradox that many of our most important discoveries about ourselves and our world are made during times of relaxation and reverie, periods when our minds and hearts are most receptive to the mysteries that surround us. We could say that the Church stands for the principle of rest in human life, the need to come apart and be quiet and open ourselves to the strange silences of God.

The secret is again one of balance. A healthy life is a balanced rhythm of work and rest, activity and contemplation, and it is important to remember that as we come to think about the sin of sloth. Each of the deadly sins is something good in itself that has been misdirected and over-emphasised, and the same distortion rules here. Sloth is the instinct for rest and creative idling taken and distorted into an unattractive passivity. We must not confuse sloth with simple physical laziness or love of sleep. They may, indeed, be signs of sloth, but they are only aspects of a sin that can be extremely subtle in its ramifications.

The real root of sloth lies in the will; it is there that the attack is made, and when it takes over it can affect everything. The will is the active, executive part of our nature. Sloth is a disease of the will. It spreads insidiously, quietly paralysing and numbing the will so that, after a while, almost any effort in any direction is too much trouble. We are not meant to drift through life like corks in a river. We are meant, under God, to take our lives into our own hands and direct and drive them by the discipline and direction of our wills. Sloth undermines this programme, constantly tempting us just to let things drift along, doing only enough to get by, making nothing of ourselves and contributing nothing to others, bobbing gently along on the surface of life, amiably and without purpose. Slothful people are rarely bad people; they rarely have enough energy to be bad and so they are often protected against some of the more active vices. Even so, they do something that can be as bad as active vice; they create the conditions in which real wickedness can flourish, because they cannot be bothered to do anything about it. Edmund Burke said that the only thing required for the triumph of evil was for good men to do nothing. It is sloth that prepares the way for great wickedness, by allowing evil and energetic people to make the running. This is the meaning of those famous words in Yeats's poem, *The Second Coming*. 'The best lack all conviction, while the worst are full of passionate intensity'.

There are three forms or modes of sloth. First of all, there is mental sloth. Those who have given in to this never find out anything for themselves. They are too lazy to inform themselves. They live on second or third hand opinions. They trot out the clichés they absorb from television and newspaper, because they cannot be bothered to arrive at opinions of their own. They do not want to make the effort that examination of the evidence requires, so they become sitting ducks for the opinion formers, the arbiters of moral and intellectual fashion in our society. Unconsciously, they absorb their ideas, their opinions, and they end as convenient statistics in those shifts of public opinion that are frequently adduced by those who stand to profit by them. Of course, there has been no real shift; there has been manipulation of public opinion in the interest, frequently commercial, of a tiny minority who are full of passionate intensity. So we must beware of second hand opinions; they are symptoms of mental sloth. We must apply our own minds to the issues of the day. Our minds are usually better than we think they are if only we'll use them, inform them by a constant exercise of intelligent discrimination.

Related to mental sloth is moral sloth. This is failure to act in situations of moral danger, either private or public. We can complain and complain about some great social evil, but be too lazy to do anything about it; too lazy to join a political party or pressure group; too lazy to do anything, because we leave it to some other agency—the government, the politically committed, 'the people who understand these things'. The danger of moral sloth can be private as well as public. We may be allowing ourselves to drift into a state of moral indifference; some bad habit may be taking over, something inimical to our soul's health. Or it may be a general hardening of our attitudes, a closing up of our hearts against those who have a legitimate claim on our compassion. Again, 'we can't be bothered' to make the effort to shake off the danger; insidiously it creeps up on us, paralyzing the will.

Finally, there is spiritual sloth. When I was

at theological college we used to call it 'the doom', that terrible weight of spiritual apathy that washes over us, so that almost everything becomes too much trouble: we cannot be bothered to pray; and even going to church demands an enormous effort. Almost anything that pertains to the spiritual quest becomes too much trouble and nothing we do seems, anyway, to make much difference— so why bother? Most people know the feeling. It is sloth rather than positive apostasy that lies behind all the statistics of decline that figure in the annual reports of most churches. If it takes over it can complete that slow strangulation of the will that is the final result of sloth. Submitting to sloth is like falling asleep in a snow drift—it spells doom.

Apart from noticing that there is a genuine need for all men and women to pace themselves through life, leaving plenty of space for reflection, rest, contemplation, what else can be said in support of sloth? The slothful can be pleasant and amiable and they do not interfere in the lives of others; they have the easy tolerance of the half-asleep, but it is this sluggish pleasantness that allows the energy of the wicked to triumph. A certain degree of laziness is a desirable attribute in a politician for a perfectly obvious reason. As a class politicians have an obsessive passion for interfering in the lives of individuals and institutions, and the more principled and conscientious they are, the more likely are they to be given to constant interventions in the life of society. Bureaucrats suffer from a similar impulse. In our society there is plenty of evidence of the effects of these energetic intrusions in almost every area of life. That is why professional politicians are a breed to be watched, no matter what their party. They are licensed to meddle in our affairs and the only thing that is likely to save us from their attentions is a saving dash of sloth, the perfectly human longing to relax and not take it all too seriously. So sloth ought to be encouraged in politicians, including the ecclesiastical variety, but the rest of us ought to flee it. If we let it enter the system it will spread insidiously, poisoning everything, leaving us jaded and indifferent. Ultimately it will paralyse the will completely so that action no longer becomes possible even if, too late, we try to summon up enough energy to break out of the trap we have built round ourselves.

The only answer to sloth is action; the steady and persistent application of the will, aided by God, to the duties that lie before us.

PART TWO

The Seven Gifts of the Holy Spirit

FEAR

On a wet Sunday one Summer I went to church in Salisbury. The church, a beautifully light and airy building, was medieval, but the service, a Family Eucharist, was pleasantly modern, like thousands of others held up and down the country at the same hour. The holy table stood outside the chancel, and the service was divided up in the modern way to maximise participation between ordained and lay members of the congregation. The sermon was thoughtful and straightforward. The whole tone of the service, while not exactly stirring, was gently Anglican. There was no sense of captivating awe or overwhelming emotion of any sort, everything was decent and orderly, nothing to set the blood racing. And high above this quiet activity soared the chancel arch, and over the arch there was a medieval Doom Painting. While we exchanged the kiss of peace with good natured self-consciousness, demons with long, forked tails were thrusting tormented souls into Hell 'where the worm does not die, and the fire is not quenched.' I returned to that painting repeatedly as the service proceeded, and the incongruity of it all struck me with considerable force. There was clearly little or no relationship between what was happening below and what was happening above. Once there would have been a solid connection between what was done or said in that church and the gruesome painting that dominated the entrance to the sanctuary. It had issued a warning:

Remember, Christian Soul,
that thou hast this day and every day of
    thy life
God to glorify
Jesus to imitate
A soul to save
A body to mortify
Sins to repent of
Virtues to acquire
Hell to avoid
Heaven to gain
Eternity to prepare for
Time to profit by
Neighbours to edify
The world to despise
Devils to combat
Passions to subdue
Judgement to undergo.

It all seems a long time ago, but that is only because we have short memories. I have known several people who felt sure they were damned, and the fires of hell are still banked regularly in certain Christian pulpits, though not, perhaps, in most Anglican churches. One of the most vivid descriptions of hell comes in one of the classic novels of this century. In *A Portrait of the Artist as a Young Man,* James Joyce recalls a sermon he heard in his youth in which the torments of hell were meticulously described.

The torment of fire is the greatest torment to which the tyrant has ever subjected his fellow creatures. Place your finger for a moment in the flame of a candle and you will feel the pain of fire. But our earthly fire was created by God for the benefit of man, to maintain in him the spark of life and to help him in the useful arts, whereas the fire of hell is of another quality and was created by God to torture and punish the unrepentant sinner. Our earthly fire also consumes more or less rapidly according as the object which it attacks is more or less combustible, so that human ingenuity has even succeeded in inventing chemical preparations to check or frustrate its action. But the sulphurous brimstone which burns in hell is a substance which is specially designed to burn for ever and for ever with unspeakable fury. Moreover, our earthly fire destroys at the same time as it burns, so that the more intense it is the shorter is its duration; but the fire of hell has this property, that it preserves that which it burns, and, though it rages with incredible intensity, it rages for ever.

Our earthly fire again, no matter how

fierce or widespread it may be, is always of a limited extent; but the lake of fire in hell is boundless, shoreless and bottomless. And this terrible fire will not afflict the bodies of the damned only from without, but each lost soul will be a hell unto itself, the boundless fire raging in its very vitals. O, how terrible is the lot of those wretched beings! The blood seethes and boils in the veins, the brains are boiling in the skull, the heart in the breast glowing and bursting, the bowels a red-hot mass of burning pulp, the tender eyes flaming like molten balls.

(Penguin edition, pp 121, 122)

It is not difficult to imagine the effect of a sermon like that on a congregation of adolescent boys. It would build an overwhelming fear into them; the very thing it was intended to do. Fear was the great preventive medicine against sin. Why risk eternal torment for the sake of a few passing pleasures? An Oxford don of the last century is reported to have warned his audience of young men against the sins of the flesh by crying out, 'Why risk your eternal soul for the sake of a pleasure, which, I am reliably informed, lasts less than ninety seconds?' So fear acted as a restraint upon sin, but it also promoted evangelical zeal. Many of the greatest missionary saints in Christian history were prompted to their heroic labours by the sombre knowledge that only their offer of the Christian gospel stood between their listeners and eternal damnation. Promoting the fear of hell in people was part of the stock-in-trade of the successful evangelist, which may be why the liberal churches that have closed down Hell are shrinking, while the churches that still invest in it are prospering.

There can be no doubt that the doctrine of Hell and the inculcation of fear are unfashionable aspects of traditional Christianity. They belong to the furniture of a bygone era and they do not fit into the small and unembellished apartments of modern Christians. The prevailing theme in contemporary theology is a naturalising of traditional Christian doctrines so that they become metaphors for the day to day struggles of ordinary people. According to that system Hell is only to be used as a metaphor for the pain and isolation that absolute selfishness brings, and fear is only respectable as a gentle warning against conduct likely to be injurious to our mental health. The trouble with that way of de-mythologizing Hell is that it does not really convince. The most persuasive part of the old teaching was its unfalsifiability in this life: the rewards and punishments came later—you might get away with something all your life, but you would not get away with it for ever. The only way to test the claim was to die, but by then it might be too late, so prudence seemed the safest course, and a determination to be confessed and shriven before departing for eternity. An important element in the plot of Shakespeare's *Hamlet* is concerned with this very system. The horrifying thing about the murder of Hamlet's father was its suddenness, rendering him incapable of that crucial act of contrition that made the difference between Heaven and Hell.

> Cut off even in the blossoms of my sin,
> Unhousel'd, disappointed, unanel'd,
> No reckoning made, but sent to my account
> With all my imperfections on my head:
> O, horrible! O, horrible! most horrible!

Hell was effective because it was one of the *last* things and its existence was provable or disprovable only beyond death. That is the essential brilliance of the idea. Like the existence of God it can only be verified eschatalogically, and by the time you are sure, it may be too late. It is this enigmatic quality that gives Hell its greatest power. Presumably if Hell exists it does not matter who believes in it, because it will have the last laugh anyway. Meanwhile it is happy to wait. And it is the very simplicity of the idea that makes it difficult to demythologise or turn into a metaphor for the loneliness that accompanies selfishness or the guilt that accompanies wickedness, because history is full of examples of wicked people who flourish like green bay trees and of selfish people who never seem smitten with self-doubt. Virtue may be its own reward and Hell may be the reward of the wicked after death, but it is manifestly not always the case that evil acts are punished in this life. I have more than a sneaking feeling, as a matter of fact, that it was this very recognition that life is unequal in its distribution of rewards and punishments that led to the creation of Hell, the place where the record was really straightened out and all the balances redressed: 'Son, remember that you in your lifetime received your good things, and Lazarus in like manner evil things, but now he is comforted here, and you are in anguish.' (Luke 16.25) Far, therefore, from being cunning devices to keep the unprivileged in their places, Heaven and Hell can be seen as radical and revolutionary in their ultimate effect, casting down the mighty from their seat, exalting the humble and meek and establishing, at last, the reign of justice.

I am aware, of course, that I am begging the question, but I think it is worth staying with the question a little longer. If the universe is meaningless and morally absurd, then the question is closed anyway. Things are the way they are and very little can be done to iron out inequalities, and the melancholy fact is that monsters of depravity and wickedness get away with it all too often. The notion that one day there will be a reckoning, that one day righteousness will be vindicated, is only a sentimental projection of what the fair-minded feel ought to happen. That is another way of begging the question, though it does not entirely rule out moral effort. We can do something here and now to protect the weak and curtail the depredations of the wicked, but it is only as a drop of water in the ocean, it does nothing to justify the torture and murder of a single child, to say nothing of the organized depravity of the Third Reich or the disorganized brutality of Amin's Uganda. In an absurd universe there is absolutely no reason why we should be surprised at anything. Moral indignation in the face of great evil, while humanly understandable, is as futile as raging against the pitiless vagaries of nature. That is one way of begging the question, but there has always been another and it is just as, if not more, compelling.

If we believe there is purpose in life and a moral structure to the universe, then the existence of unrequited evil presents us with a problem. What is the use of law if it cannot be vindicated, what is the point of a God whose rule can be so easily mocked? One answer to the problem is the hypothesis of Hell. We can, I think, confidently jettison the descriptions of the infernal region lovingly detailed by hell-fire preachers, and we can be equally sure that our forefathers over-populated Hell with petty sinners in much the same way that they sent them to the antipodes, but I do not think we can so easily dispose of Hell as at least an important hypothesis. We may be tempted to dismiss the doctrine of Hell as an example of the moral barbarity of our forefathers, but we ought to consider the matter a little more carefully. Each generation in history is selective in its pursuit of virtue and in its commitment to truth, and just as each generation imagines itself to be more intelligent than the one that went before it, and wiser than the one that comes after it, so it imagines itself to be more virtuous than both its predecessors and successors.

In fact, we all pick and choose. There are fashionable virtues as well as fashionable vices, though we usually only notice the vices of our forebears. We may be more merciful than our forefathers, but we have surely lost something of their robustness, and one of our vices may well be moral cowardice in the face of evil. I am certainly offended by the avidity with which certain types of religious people describe Hell and insist on its reality, but human beings and their ideas of value do tend towards hypertrophy, so that they often end by caricaturing themselves and inflating their ideas to absurd and often frightening proportions. The Irish Catholic sermon quoted by James Joyce is a good example of this tendency, with its confident description of an absolutely unknowable situation. One of the tragic things about this tendency to hypertrophy, apart from its elaboration of spare and severe theories into philosophical structures of Byzantine complexity, is that it almost guarantees the rejection of the truth concealed beneath the complexity by the subsequent generation, which, in its turn, over-develops the opposing truth, until a succeeding generation jerks the pendulum back.

If our forefathers seemed to exaggerate the wrath of God and the fate of sinners, our generation seems to have fallen into the opposite trap of so emphasising the mercy of God and the complexity of human nature as to reduce the moral struggle to insignificance. There is something most peculiar about a spiritual tradition that can offer such contrasting estimates of a casual act of copulation, for instance, one generation seeing it as imperilling the eternal salvation of the participants, while a succeeding generation can hardly summon enough indignation to raise its eyebrows. To a generation with no tolerance for and little understanding of human weakness, the concept of Hell will be used like a bludgeon to keep people in order. And it is this we find most offensive, and some of us know how damaging it can be to weak human beings. An American psychiatrist told me that he was appalled at the psychological damage he constantly came across among traditional Irish Catholics, many of them guilt-ridden and fearful, especially about their sexuality, but he was reluctant to say so publicly because it was the Catholic Church that kept him in business.

So it is not surprising that we reject the concept of Hell and play down the biblical notion of the justice of God, except when it is convenient to us to turn it against our political opponents. It is not surprising that we have done this, but is it wise? Can we afford to dispense with the concept of Hell and the experience of fear in the moral and spiritual life? Uncongenial as it may be to the modern consciousness, Hell is firmly rooted in biblical religion, including the New Testament, and it seems to be an important conviction in all the great monotheistic religions. Certainly Buddhism affirms the continuity of moral consequences in its doctrine of the transmigration of souls, each successive life being determined by the total moral result of the preceding life. And in Zoroastrianism a doctrine of strict retribution was taught.

I do not think it is profitable to spectulate on the exact fate of those who have chosen evil rather than good, but there can be no doubt that Jesus taught that final rejection by God was at least a theoretical possibility: 'I tell you, my friends, do not fear those who kill the body, and after that have no more that they can do. But I will warn you whom to fear: fear him who, after he has killed, has power to cast into hell; yes, I tell you, fear him!' (Luke 12.4-5). But we do not need to depend exclusively upon the testimony of revealed religion for this conclusion. Our own reason, untainted by sentimentality or moral cowardice, should guide us to a similar judgement. If there is a God at the heart of reality, a holy and righteous God, and if it is our destiny to grow into his likeness by the consent of our wills and the operation of his grace, then it must be possible for free creatures to reject that destiny, to refuse good and choose evil, and the consequences of those actions must be our own willed rejection of God, whether for eternity or only for a time.

Søren Kierkegaard said that God did not become man in order to make trivial remarks. The Incarnation was the climax of a long tradition of divine beseeching in which God sought to warn and persuade his children of the issues at stake in the struggles of earthly life. Far from being a vengeful God, he goes to every length short of total obliteration of human freedom in order to warn us and guide us, rising up early and sending prophets and wise men, and finally coming among us in the form of man, his word of longing and warning made flesh. And that is not all, for the crucifixion of Jesus Christ can be seen as God's last desperate attempt to get our attention, to warn us of the fatefulness of our choices. But in none of this is there a repudiation of our sovereign freedom to reject goodness and God, and make evil our good and our God. If there is a moral structure to the universe, therefore, and if every allowance is made for circumstance and weakness and diminished responsibility (and we can be quite sure that the God of Jesus Christ goes to extraordinary lengths, again short of violating our freedom, to help us choose life), it must follow that we ought to bear the responsibility of our free choices, and part of that freedom must be the possibility of rejecting God and his goodness. Philosophers continue to speculate about the possible nature of that condition of willed rejection of God. In *Faith and Reason,* for instance, Richard Swinburne writes:

. . . there seem to be various possible states for those who have finally rejected the good. They might cease to exist after death. They might cease to exist after suffering some limited physical pain as part of the punishment of their wickedness. Or they might continue to exist forever pursuing trivial pursuits (as amusingly depicted in Bernard Shaw's *Man and Superman*), perhaps not even realizing that the pursuits were trivial.

(p. 172)

However you describe it, the testimony of most religion and much philosophy is that we are engaged in a struggle and the outcome is momentous for good or ill. But it is probably pointless to spend much time on a consideration of the abstract question of eternal punishment. There are, of course, both social and philosophical consequences to all Christian doctrine, but the best use the individual can make of them is to apply them to the realities of his or her own life. The fate of the great villains of history is certainly an interesting speculation, but my destiny and the effect of my choices upon it is not a speculative question, it is a profoundly personal one. Christ does not call us to a life of joyless guilt in which we are constantly looking over our shoulders for the approach of the divine watchdog, but he does call us to a life of moral seriousness, a life in which we are making or unmaking our souls, a life in which there should be a measure of fear of one who will not deny us the tragic dignity of choosing to go to hell if we so will it. He will die for us, but he will not abrogate our freedom, even if it means losing us forever. A god who loves us enough to die for us in the person of the Divine Son, and who respects us enough to let us reject him, perhaps for ever, is a god to be in awe of. In him we confront absolute love and absolute justice, and the combination is terrifying to our trivial and complacent souls. It can be no accident that the closer the mystics and seers have drawn to God, the more intimately related they become, the more awed and overwhelmed they are. God, it seems, is a consuming fire. The closer we draw to him, the more dread and fascination we feel. The paradox would seem to follow that if we feel no danger in our approach to God, it is probably because we are very far away from the fire.

PIETY and KNOWLEDGE

A Japanese theologian, now working in the United States of America, told me some years ago that he did not think anyone could understand the essence of biblical religion unless he uprooted himself from his native soil and went to live in an alien land. The theme of exile is persistent in both the Old and New Testaments, from Abraham going out not knowing whither he went, through the experience of exile by the waters of Babylon, right up to the recognition in the Letter to the Hebrews that here we have no abiding city. This exile theme stresses the conditional and uncertain nature of all human experience and promotes the disposition of detachment from all earthly things, emphasising that human beings are pilgrims and travellers, not settlers. It is an important and obvious theme and detachment is an important virtue, but it is not the only lesson to be learnt from the experience of exile. Exiles may well use their homesickness as a parable for heaven's longing, but they are even more likely to use it as a spur to remembrance.

Blows the wind today, and the sun and the
    rain are flying,

Blows the wind on the moors today and
   now
Where about the graves of the martyrs the
   whaups are crying,
   My heart remembers how!

Grey recumbent tombs of the dead in desert
   places,
   Standing-stones on the vacant wine-red
   moor,
Hills of sheep, and the howes of the silent
   vanished races,
   And winds, austere and pure.

Be it granted me to behold you again in dying,
   Hills of home! and to hear again the call;
Hear about the graves of the martyrs the
   peewee crying,
   And hear no more at all.   *(R. L. Stevenson)*

The experience of exile lends a keenness to
memory, framing the dear, remembered place
in the mind's eye. Any exile knows the sud-
den pricking of regret occasioned by the
arrival of a month old newspaper from home
or a cheap calendar of photographs of blue
remembered hills.

But exile is not just a spatial experience,
the fact of distance from one's homeland;
chronological exile is just as potent, the
experience of lost time and a longing for the
dear, dead past. Many of the great autobio-
graphical novels are woven round this theme

of searching for the meaning of the past, the significance of the way we were. Many experience their mature selves as somehow exiled from their early lives, which they lived heedlessly without noticing, without regard. So they comb through their memories to find, in Tom Wolfe's language, 'the lost lane-end into heaven, a shore, a leaf, an unfound door.' They look back into the well of time to discover the faces they have loved long since and lost awhile. Saul Bellow in *Humboldt's Gift* puts it like this:

Listen here, do you remember when we moved to Chicago from Appleton and lived in those dark rooms on Rice Street? And you were an obese boy and I a thin boy? And Mama doted on you with black eyes, and Papa flew into a fit because you dunked your bread in the cocoa? And before he escaped into the wood business he slaved in the bakery, the only work he could find, a gentleman but labouring at night? And came home and hung his white overalls behind the bathroom door so that the can always smelled like a bakeshop and the stiff flour fell off in scales? And he slept handsome and angry, on his side all day, with one hand under his face and the other between his drawn-up knees? While Mama boiled the wash on the coal-stove, and you and I disappeared to school? Do you remember all that? Well, I'll tell you why I bring it up – there are good aesthetic reasons why this should not be wiped from the record eternally. No one would put so much heart into things doomed to be forgotten and wasted. Or so much love. Love is gratitude for being. This love would be hate, Ulick, if the whole thing was nothing but a cheat.

What geographical and chronological exile produce is a type of piety, an affectionate reverence for the things lost. Piety is a kind of fondness or love, a recognition of what you owe the land that bred you or the parents who bore you. Some people feel it more towards certain places, hills they remember or corners of a landscape; for others it is towards the immediate community, the street or village or neighbourhood. For many it is more abstracted than that and has something to do with the gathered history and experience of a whole nation, the kind of piety we call patriotism. Patriotism is vaguely unfashionable today and Dr Johnson did well to remind us that it could be the refuge of scoundrels, but it is a carping and irritable mind that only sees the shadow cast by a particular virtue. Just as it often takes the experience of exile to induce a proper affection for our homeland, so it often takes some great threat to the homeland before we become aware of the deep love we have for it. Harold Nicolson discovered the depth of his patriotism, his love for Britain, during the London Blitz. Rupert Hart-Davis provides us with an interesting sidelight on Nicolson's patriotism in a letter to George Lyttelton. He wrote:

What, if anything, makes you cry? I asked Harold Nicolson this question at the Literary Society dinner, and he said: 'Three things only–patriotism, injustice righted, and misunderstanding explained. Tragedy never'. I agree whole-heartedly about patriotism: I can't see the Queen on a newsreel without a lump in my throat; but am less sure about the other two. (Volume V, p. 37)

The lump that some people get in their throats on the last night of the Proms and at certain other types of national celebration is an example of natural piety or reverence. It is what the psychologists call an affective state: the contemplation of the beloved group or symbol of the homeland produces an emotional response, a welling up of positive feeling. Affective states can be negative or positive. Fear is an affective state, but it is an example of negative affectivity. Here the emotional response is of dread or anxiety, and we have seen that it will be present in any approach to God that is honest and fully aware. But negative affectivity, the emotion of fear, is not the only appropriate response to God. The book of Ecclesiasticus cautions us:

You who fear the Lord, wait for his mercy; and turn not aside, lest you fall. 2.7.

In other words, Fear is highly appropriate in our approach to God but it must not be the only or the main emotional response we feel. A faith that is built on fear will, sooner or later, turn aside and fall. Our relationship with God will always be tinged with fear, there will always be some element of awe and dread in it, but a religion of exclusively negative affectivity is as distorted as the sort of breezy attitude that approaches God as though we had gone to school with him. So the writer of Ecclesiasticus exhorts those who feel dread in God's presence to wait for his mercy, wait for the revealing of the side of his nature that induces piety rather than fear, affection rather than anxiety. He tells us that we must keep these two emotions in balance because they correspond to something in the nature of God which we experience as a sort of duality, whereas it is really the effect of his unity upon our confused nature, because 'as his majesty is, so also is his mercy' (2.18). The majesty, the tremendousness of God evokes fear, but equal to God's majesty is his mercy, and that evokes piety or sheer fondness. Waiting for the disclosure of the mercy of God involves the kind of contemplation that we saw operating in the case of the exile who calls to mind the beauties of his home-land. The gift of piety is the gift of affectionate regard or remembrance, it is a kind of patriotism felt towards God. Corresponding to the exile's brooding upon memories of the homeland is the believer's meditating on the mercy and kindness of God. One of the most potent stimulants to this sort of piety is a meditation on the Parable of the Prodigal Son, found in the fifteenth chapter of St Luke's gospel.

There are three main characters in the story, the father and his two sons, but the focus is on the loving constancy of the father. Each of the sons abuses the love of the father, the younger son by going into the far land and wasting his father's gift, the older of the two by a dour and grudging obedience that did the right things for the wrong reasons. Most types of human frailty are contained within the range that stretches between these two brothers. The younger son represents the human tendency to excess and destructive self-indulgence, whereas the older son shows us a kind of emotional meanness and lack of generosity. Each weakness has its own corresponding strength: profligates are often compassionate and understanding of human weakness, while puritans are usually disciplined and steadfast. In fact, each needs to learn from the other, the prodigal learning something about endurance and obedience from his brother, while he, in turn, ought to capture something of the openness and daring that characterised his younger brother. Each gets his relationship with his father wrong. The wild young man pushes his father's love for him to the ultimate test, while his sober and steadfast brother seems to have no sense of that love and its graciousness, seeing everything in contractual terms with nothing of the freedom and generosity and imprudence of real love.

Each had to learn a wonderful and liberating lesson about the father's love: it is constant and unwavering and needs only to be turned to. The younger son 'came to himself' and went home to his father's arms, and the older brother's complaint was heard and replied to with disarming graciousness. The prodigal son and his brother were both humbled by the kindness and mercy of their father, so unlike their own self-absorption. The story ends with the father's gentle admonition to his first-born son, but there is no reason why we should not go on to add a final scene of our own devising in which the two brothers unite in gratitude and admiration of their father, forgetting their own conflicts and failures in sheer thankfulness.

This spirit of gratitude is one of the wellsprings of religion and it adds grace and generosity towards those who have it. The key-note of piety is gratitude for sins forgiven and weaknesses understood, based on the astonished recognition that 'as his majesty is, so also is his mercy'. And this gratefulness leads to another characteristic of piety, which is its courtesy, its ceremoniousness. Just as patriots express their patriotism in act and gesture, such as standing for the national anthem, or enlisting in the forces when their nation is attacked, so do the pious show their gratitude to God by certain acts and observances. Part of this is the natural and spontaneous reflex of the grateful person to the giver of some great gift, but some of it is based on a more subtle psychological principle. One of the purposes of ceremony is the inculcation of the disposition it is meant to express: acts that are meant to express patriotism also serve to increase and encourage patriotism. Showing love to others can also serve to increase the very love we feel. W. B. Yeats captured this insight in the last stanza of his poem. *A Prayer for my Daughter:*

> . . . and may her bridegroom bring her to a
>   house
> Where all's accustomed, ceremonious;
> For arrogance and hatred are the wares
> Peddled in the thoroughfares.
> How but in custom and in ceremony
> Are innocence and beauty born?
> Ceremony's a name for the rich horn,
> And custom for the spreading laurel tree.

Down the ages the pious have known this to be true. In their observances 'all's accustomed, ceremonious', from devout uses such as the sign of the cross right up to fasting and alms-giving and the use of retreats and other methods of devotion. Prudent believers do not spurn these opportunities for customary piety, knowing that, in addition to expressing devotion to God, they actually increase it. Piety, then, is our full-hearted response to the graciousness of God whose nature is always to have mercy and who declares his almighty power most chiefly in showing mercy and pity. Meditating on that divine tenderness both expresses and increases piety.

The third gift of the Holy Spirit may appear to be a strange intruder in what is largely a series of dispositions. It is the gift of Know-ledge, but it is well placed after Fear and Piety because, in one sense, it is the balanced recognition that both of these dispositions are correct and necessary attributes of any mature spirituality. One of the signs of an immature spirituality is an imbalance, a dis-torted emphasis upon one aspect of God's nature at the expense of other aspects. Chris-tianity is a spirituality of paradox that stresses the apparent contraries in our knowledge of God. The Letter to the Hebrews tells us that God is a consuming fire and we feel an entirely appropriate dread and awe in his presence. If this side of our knowledge of God is absent our knowledge is partial and immature, but if it is all we know then it is equally unbalanced, because it has ignored the equally important emphasis upon the mercy and loving-kindness of God. Nor are we to fluctuate wildly between dread and fondness in our approach to God. Each must be held in balance with the other, so that we feel a most tender dread towards God or a sort of fearful but absolute affection for him. In other words, the gift of Knowledge brings us to a true awareness of the richness and completeness of the nature of God and it rescues us from a monocular preoccupation with only one aspect of his being. The presence of Fear and Piety, Awe and Affection are both essential to true Knowledge, for 'as is his majesty, so also is his mercy'.

COURAGE

Mark Twain once said that it was not the bits of the Bible he did not understand that bothered him, but the bits he did understand. There is much in both testaments to console us in the face of suffering and death. As I have already pointed out, there is much comfort in the words of Jesus, but there is a lot that disturbs us. Jesus seems to offer us absolute consolation, yet he seems to call us to absolute sacrifice. After a while we learn to live with the great impossible commands by muffling or diffusing them, by deflecting them so that they do not really get through to us. Most Christians, unless they are totally deluded about themselves, know that they do this, know that there is an enormous gap between what they profess with their lips and what they do with their lives. I think that gap is inescapable, but the way we try to bridge it can be significant. A few try to bridge the gap by following lives that cost them, in Eliot's phrase, 'not less than everything'. They find the courage to obey Christ, no matter what it costs them. There are others, however, who try to naturalise or minimise the radical challenge of Christ. They close the gap, not by reaching beyond themselves to Christ, but by pulling Christ towards them and adapting him to their own uses.

None of this surprises me, though I am always moved when I discover Christians who follow Christ at considerable cost to themselves. Most of us do not attempt radical discipleship. We allow Christ to modify our actions somewhat, to influence our attitudes, but we know that is far from the kind of discipleship that really makes a difference. The only virtue we possess in this situation is a sort of rueful modesty, a mild shame that we are not particularly heroic. This sort of self-deprecatory discipleship has much to be said for it but it can breed a kind of uncomfortable comfort all of its own, an inverted complacence that thanks God it is very much as other men are. That is why it is important to go on meditating on the tradition, on the story of Jesus. Human transformation, which is one of the purposes of the Church, is an agonizingly slow process, but it won't happen at all unless we dispose ourselves at least to the possibility of change, and that means, at least in part, opening ourselves to the whole range of Christian experience; demand as well as consolation, challenge as well as comfort.

Sometimes we ought to meditate on the uncomfortable words of Jesus. One of the most uncomfortable and discouraging parts of the tradition is found in Luke's Gospel. In chapter nine we find our Lord on his way up to Jerusalem, setting his face towards his own destiny, striding up to the Holy City to die. We can sense a concentration in him, a loneliness, an austerity, a severity, a kind of overwhelming courage that makes us whimper with anxiety and disbelief, because we don't feel very brave and don't want him to trouble us, to make demands upon us, to upset the unadventurous tenor of our lives. Speaking quite personally, I prefer the Jesus of the theological discourses or the teasing, elliptical parables, something I can *think* about. In fact, I like to *think* about Jesus. I like theology. I like giving my mind a metaphysical work-out. That is the kind of stuff I eat up. I like Jesus in my study between the covers of a book. I like the Jesus of the lecture hall, as scholars wrestle with what he means. I do not like this Jesus who is going up to Jerusalem, with his face stern and his eyes burning and his manner curt, rejecting the approaches of three men who were interested in becoming his disciples, joining his study group, learning from him.

When the days drew near for him to be received up, he set his face to go to Jerusalem. As they were going along the road, a man said to him, 'I will follow you wherever you go'. And Jesus said to him, 'Foxes have holes, and birds of the air have nests; but the Son of man has nowhere to lay his head'. To another he said, 'Follow me'. But he said, 'Lord, let me first go and bury my father'. But he said to him, 'Leave the dead to bury their own dead; but as for you, go and proclaim the kingdom of God'. Another said, 'I will follow you, Lord; but let me first say farewell to those at my home'. Jesus said to him, 'No one who puts his hand to the plough and looks back is fit for the kingdom of God'.

(Luke 9.51, 57-62)

That kind of absolutism makes us anxious and wistful and ashamed, because we are sure that we do not possess the kind of high courage that is demanded. We admire courage in others, however. Whenever I read this passage from Luke I am irresistibly reminded of King Henry's great speech in Shakespeare's Henry V.

He which hath no stomach to this fight,
Let him depart; his passport shall be made,
And crowns for convoy put into his purse;
We would not die in that man's company
That fears his fellowship to die with us.
For he today that sheds his blood with me
Shall be my brother; be he ne'er so vile
This day shall gentle his condition:
And gentlemen in England, now a-bed
Shall think themselves accursed they were
    not here,
And hold their manhood cheap whiles any
    speaks

That fought with us upon Saint Crispin's
day.

(Act IV. iii)

There are always some who rise to the
summons of the trumpet and there are
always others, 'gentlemen in England, now
a-bed', who do not. Sometimes, years later,
they hold their manhood cheap, because it
has never been tried or tested. It lay a-bed on
Crispin's day. Now, I know that Christianity is
a large thing and that there is room in it for
cowards, but I think it is important to know
what you are as you seek, in some way, to follow Jesus. And Jesus does not always console
or stimulate us; sometimes he sets his face
like a flint and strides off to Jerusalem to die.
In passages like this we confront an inescapable side of the message of Jesus: his demand
for absolute, unconditional commitment; his
call for a wild and unselfregarding heroism
that spurns even the most tender and sacred
bonds of our humanity. If we want to be
honest to the whole gospel, we must confront passages like this and hear what they
say, even though they burn us and sear us
and overwhelm us with that special kind of
loneliness that God's call sometimes induces.
Let us look at what happened during that
swift and final journey to Jerusalem. Three
men approach Jesus and offer to join his
band. Jesus, unlike many other pastors who
are trying to build up their congregations,

tries to make it as difficult as he can. He more or less refuses them, turns them down. He does not try to adjust his message or otherwise accommodate himself to them. He makes it hard: 'Foxes have holes and birds of the air have nests, but if you follow me abandon every impulse towards comfort and security, abandon your attempts to maintain your standard of living or improve it; if you will follow me I must come first, and I am the homeless Christ, more homeless, even, than the wild beasts. If you follow me you cannot tack me on to your life like a spare-time interest. I want you totally. There is nothing you should want more than me. If you don't have that kind of radical commitment, go back home, back to that security you have carefully built up.' And Jesus left him standing there on the dusty road as he strode up the hill. The man watched him reach the bend in the road and he never looked back, so he turned slowly back to the village, now strangely dead to him, back to the other gentlemen now a-bed.

The next applicant had aged parents whose affairs he wanted to put in order. 'Let me return and make arrangements for my father who is dying; I'll meet you soon.' And then Jesus produces that harsh and terrible saying: 'Let the dead, the spiritually indifferent, the ones with blank eyes and no high longings in their hearts, let them look after the dead. If you would be mine, come now, this moment; for you this is the time.' Apparently, you cannot follow Christ and allow your family or nation or party or set or class any priority over him. He has to come first. He demands a loyalty that abrogates all other loyalties. So Jesus left him standing there on the dusty road as he strode up the hill. The man watched Jesus reach the top of the hill and disappear from view, and he never looked back, so he turned slowly back to the village, now strangely small and narrow to him, and joined the other gentlemen now a-bed.

But the third applicant would surely get in. All he wanted to do was to dash back to say goodbye and pick up another pair of sandals. 'Do not look back', says Jesus, 'come now, now. No one who puts his hand to the plough and looks back is fit for the kingdom of God.' And the man would know what he was talking about. He was a farmer. When ploughing you have to look straight ahead at your point. If you look back you will make a crooked furrow. Having Jesus in our sights is the same. We are not to look back over our shoulder at what we have left behind, at where we have been and what we have seen. There is to be no dangerous sanctifying of the past and its memories: Jesus is up ahead of us. If we keep our eyes on him we shall be in direct continuity with the past anyway, because he has always been the fixed point that recedes before us. So he told the third man, 'Do not go back or even look back. Do not repine. Come. Now.' But he, too, was left standing on the dusty road as Jesus strode with terrible determination to that appointment in Jerusalem. So he slowly went back into the village, back through the fields to the sleeping village where everyone lay a-bed.

What are we to make of this frightening series of encounters? Well, we could, with some legitimacy, soften them by a certain kind of interpretation. We could tell ourselves that this type of wild, unconditional commitment is asked of some but not of all. Jesus did not say this kind of thing to everyone. He left Martha and Mary in their cottage at Bethany. He let Zacchaeus keep half his goods. So these must be special cases. We do not know anything about the circumstances surrounding these encounters. We only see the last scene of the last act. Certainly, some are called to this kind of heroic commitment, but not all are, fortunately. Some are called to an extraordinary vocation, to the monastic life, for example, with its vows of poverty, celibacy and obedience, or to a life dedicated to serving the poor. It can be anything, but only those who feel the call know, because they feel the prompting in their hearts, the longing to leave all and follow Jesus. The rest of us, fortunately, are permitted to stay at home. We are not required to take the steep road to Jerusalem.

Well, there is undoubtedly some legitimacy

in that type of exegesis, but it is not entirely honest because in some sense Jesus lays an unconditional demand upon each of us. He wants some kind of wildness and extravagance and generosity from all of us. Following him requires some kind of courage, and courage is the most important virtue because without it the other virtues cannot stand for long. Some people seem to be constitutionally brave and courageous. St Paul certainly was, and so, for example, was Winston Churchill. People like that seem to seek out danger, it calls forth something in them that 'wants war, wants wounds'. In 1940 when France was defeated, Churchill, back from a visit to Bordeaux, reported to the British Cabinet that he had been unable to persuade the crumpled ally to stand. 'And so, gentlemen', he said, 'we stand alone'. There was an anxious silence and the faces round the long table were tense and strained. The man William Manchester calls 'the last lion', looked round slowly and said, 'I find it rather exhilarating'. That kind of fearlessness frequently characterises the great leader, but it is not necesarily the same thing as courage. Courage is the ability to deny your fear and weakness and make a stand. Courage feels the urge to flee but it stands fast. Christians need courage. It is important in three ways.

First of all, without it the moral life is not really possible. It takes courage to hold out against the prevailing norms of the surrounding culture. It may require courage, for example, for a Christian student to hold out against pressure from fellow students to experiment with drugs or sex. It takes courage for politicians to withstand the opportunities for corruption that confront them, especially the intellectual corruption that is more insidious than the taking of a bribe. The moral life inevitably leads to non-conformity, and there is always enormous pressure on us to conform to our group, whether it is a peer group, a social class, an ecclesiastical party or a network of friends whose approval is important to us. It requires courage to withstand the pressure to conform to the group standard.

And the same is true in our search for truth in the world of ideas. There are fashions in thought as in everything else. It requires courage to think for ourselves and not simply accept the prevailing wisdom. One of the stultifying effects of our electronic culture is the media blitz that can propagate a fashion or a personality or a political cliché in a few hours. If we study the speeches of public figures we will find that they are filled with incantatory formulae designed to procure a measure of automatic applause from the appropriate audience. Herding together, group conformity, is a strong instinct in most of us, but it is an essentially defensive reaction that can protect us against the invasion of new and unpalatable truth. Guarding old truth and being able to receive new truth both require courage.

Finally, courage is needed in the field of personal relations. Most normal people like to be liked and hate conflict, but in any institution there are always those who, consciously or unconsciously, take advantage of this situation and bully their way to the front of the line. They are usually angry people who do not mind making scenes and who feel they have a right of constant complaint. If they are faced with compliant or fearful leaders they can create permanent uproar in an institution by constant emotional bullying, the inter-personal equivalent of the revolutionary tactics of aggrieved minorities. It requires courage to confront such people and put them in their place. When they are not opposed with courage and intelligence such people, by their tactics of emotional and moral blackmail, can create havoc and take control. Our era is filled with examples of the successful effrontery of indignant pressure-groups. Every parish priest knows the experience, often to his cost, but his experience is only a miniaturisation of a permanent struggle between the majority of balanced and good natured human beings, and shifting shoals of indignant minorities who behave like piranha fish in a goldfish bowl. Great courage is needed to withstand them.

It is obvious, therefore, that courage, in

some measure, is needed by the most unspectacular and unheroic Christian disciple. There are many situations in ordinary living when it is required. Most of us know that we are not going to follow Jesus to the death in Jerusalem. We are going to stay right where we are, like those three who met him as he travelled. But maybe we can allow something of the flavour of the madness of Jesus to creep into the way we live. It may be possible to follow him and stay put at the same time. It may be possible to discover a little more moral courage in our lives, so that we do not go along with everything that is happening around us even though we have decided to stay just where we are. Maybe we can go out to others a little more generously. Most of us are too tied to our own problems and preoccupations. Let us forget them now and again and commit ourselves to something beyond ourselves. Above all, we can pray for the gift of courage, the foundation of all other virtues. Cowards can sometimes find the courage they need to meet the challenges that face them. One of the best of modern prayers, written by Bede Jarrett who knew struggle and suffering in his own life, is a prayer for courage. It might be a way to begin.

'May he give us all the courage that we need to go the way he shepherds us. That when he calls we may go unfrightened. If he bids us come to him across the waters, that

90

unfrightened we may go. And if he bids us climb the hill, may we not notice that it is a hill, mindful only of the happiness of his company. He made us for himself, that we should travel with him and see him at last, in his unveiled beauty in the abiding city where he is light and happiness and endless home.'

COUNSEL

One of the most distressing characteristics of our era is the increase in addictive behaviour. An addiction is a compulsive dependence upon some type of substance or some form of activity. Most people are aware of the more obvious types of addiction to alcohol or heroin, but there is an almost infinite range of possibilities for obsessive behaviour. Almost anything, it seems, can be an obsession to someone. The word obsession comes from the Latin verb 'besiege' and this meaning captures something of the experience very well. Those who are in the grip of an obsession feel besieged, attacked, undermined by forces beyond themselves and outside their control. The object of the dependent obsession can be almost anything, though drugs of various sorts are the obvious examples. There are other types of addictive behaviour, however, ranging from various types of erotomania or sexual dependence to comparatively harmless obsessions, such as avoiding cracks on the pavement or touching every third railing or never walking under ladders. I knew a woman who was addicted to the smell of shoe polish and got 'high' every morning cleaning her children's shoes.

Related to this type of behaviour are the

various types of phobia to which men and women can be subject. Acute fear of open places or closed-in places are the obvious examples, but almost anything can become the focus of phobic behaviour and give rise to enormous stress and anxiety. The most tragic thing about people in the grip of these various compulsions, whether positive addictions or negative aversions, is the complete undermining of their freedom to choose. Most people have a limited level of freedom in their lives, they are not totally programmed or determined by forces outside themselves, though their behaviour is radically modified by them. The person in the grip of a compulsion, however, has lost the ability to choose. Like the inhabitants of a besieged city, people who are in the grip of a compulsion are not free to come and go as they choose. Putting to one side the deadly effect of most addictions on the person's body, the most overwhelming effect is the destruction of freedom and the values it serves. The victim of an addiction is a slave driven by a tyrant to whom absolute loyalty is owed and whose rule penetrates and dominates every aspect of life.

These conditions are very difficult to cure, though strategies and therapies, with varying degrees of success, have been developed in recent years to combat them. One of the oldest approaches to one of these problems is the famous programme developed by the organization called Alcoholics Anonymous. Alcoholics Anonymous have developed what are called 'The Twelve Steps' to sobriety, but they can be distilled into three operating principles. The most obvious principle is that it is the next drink that must not be taken and that you must take the self-denial one day at a time. Even sober alcoholics know that they are only ever one drink away from disaster. The programme requires of its participants the making of a ruthlessly honest moral and spiritual self-inventory. The search for sobriety requires the abandonment of all self-delusion and the acquirement of personal responsibility. Finally, the alcoholic in the programme is encouraged to call upon God's help and guidance, in a manner consistent with the person's beliefs. Alcoholics Anonymous does not promote any particular version of belief, but implicit in its programme is the conviction that there is some power or grace in the universe that is accessible to our need and with which we ought to co-operate if we would be whole creatures.

These three operating principles provide us with all the elements in the traditional approach to Christian discipleship. Taken together they provide us with a useful method for spiritual formation. The thing being sought is an increase in human freedom and personal responsibility, freedom being perceived as the proper directing of the self towards the attainment of a balanced personality. Each element is important. It is important to live in the present by surrendering ourselves to the duties, joys and opportunities that confront us now, without vain repining over the past or anxious concern for the future. A properly balanced life will steer a passage between regret over the past and obsession with the future. One-day-at-a-time is a very good rule for the spiritual life, for which the Abbé de Caussade invented the phrase 'the sacrament of the present moment'. We are to do God's will where we are and as we are, performing the duty or avoiding the temptation that we face at the moment. For some reason this is difficult for us. The present seems to have less reality for us than the past, and the future often dominates our present consciousness. Obsession with the past, nostalgia, is seductively debilitating and should be sternly controlled.

In the dark twilight of an autumn
    morn,
I stood within a little country-town,
Wherefrom a long acquainted path went
    down
To the dear village haunts where I was
    born;
The low of oxen on the rainy wind,
Death and the Past, came up the
    well-known road,
And bathed my heart with tears, but
    stirr'd my mind

To tread once more the track so long
   untrod;
But I was warn'd. 'Regrets which are not
   thrust
Upon thee, seek not; for this sobbing
   breeze
Will but unman thee; thou art bold to
   trust
Thy woe-worn thoughts among these
   roaring trees,
And gleams of by-gone playgrounds – Is't
   no crime
To rush by night into the arms of Time?'
                    (*Charles Tennyson Turner*)

The danger of the past, of probing among regrets that are not thrust upon us, especially if we have much to be ashamed of for things done and left undone, is that it can paralyse our will to tackle with courage the time that is still left to us. And the future, too, can be a threat. We can dissipate our time with day-dreams about the future, either with ambitious fantasies or with romantic longings. We can spend the present so plotting and planning for the future that we never really live where we are at all, never mentally unpack and settle down in the here-and-now because we are constantly preparing for the next stage.

The answer to these threats lies in the second principle of the three, the need to purge ourselves of illusion and self-delusion by making, from time to time, a searching and ruthless moral and spiritual inventory of the self. We deprive the past of its power over us by the use of some form of confession. We acknowledge 'our dear time's waste', the waste of the past and the squandering of the present, and then we put the shame behind us, we do not wallow in it. And we are able to do this, able to wipe the past clean, as it were, because of the third element in our three-fold path, reliance upon the grace and guidance of God. Indeed, it is this element in the situation that enables us to deal with the others, because it is here that we recognize the power of hope. We are not, in fact, locked into any situation, because there is always a way of escape, an opening towards transcendence, however tiny and imperceptible it may be. And it is this opening, this prevalence of grace, that is our best hope, because it promises the possibility of change.

It is this third element that is identified as the gift of Counsel or Guidance. The energy of the Holy Spirit is available to us, no matter how we perceive it or conceptualize it. Christians will pray unselfconsciously for the gift of Counsel from the Holy Spirit where others will be content to rely, implicitly, on some sort of instinctive feel for the way things are and the power of positive thinking. However we conceptualize it, we are talking about the experience of grace, the experience of something beyond ourselves, some energy for good, that wills us to overcome the temptations that besiege us. We could develop a thoroughly natural way of understanding this by observing the fact, however mysterious it may be, that, to a very great extent, people make their own luck by an open and expectant and trusting attitude to life; or they make their own misfortune by a tight and defensive and suspicious attitude. Some people are undoubtedly accident prone and some people 'have the luck of the devil'. It is dangerous to generalise on this topic, but there does seem to be some principle of natural grace working here, and those who trust life are often fortunate, while those who mistrust it are often victims of the very things they dread. Christians understand this activity as co-operation with or the rejection of grace, which is the word we use to describe the operation of the Holy Spirit in our lives. By seeking guidance, asking for the gift of Counsel, we open ourselves to healing and direction and we create a fountain of hope within our souls.

Saints who live in a more or less permanent state of recollectedness, or awareness of God and his guidance, are endowed with divine counsel almost unconsciously. Like expert drivers or dancers, they operate instinctively. They have a certain 'touch' or 'feel' and if you go to them for advice you recognize this supernatural dimension in their counsel. Where it is operating under maximum conditions, that is to say, where the person is utterly surrendered to God and his guidance, the operation of this gift of counsel can be quite miraculous in its ability to penetrate to the heart of a soul's difficulties without long prior consultations. It is said that the Curé d'Ars, a famous priest in France in the last century, had this gift of insight, enabling him to counsel penitents, who came to him in their thousands, with great insight and rapidity. And people who give themselves to the ministry of counselling others are aware of ways in which, time after time, they are able to get to the root of a person's difficulties and find some modest opening for hope in the situation.

Most of us, however, have to submit ourselves to more humdrum methods as we seek to acquire the gift of Counsel, and the key to all the methods is the ability to empty ourselves to some extent of ourselves so that another may fill us. And most of us are filled through the ear, so we are called to a real discipline of listening. If we find ourselves being sought for counsel then we must listen with our whole being to the other person. We must hold back our instinct to judge or come to conclusions, waiting for the other to open out trustingly before us, a gift that will only be offered if we are felt, however unconsciously, to be open and generous in our attitude. Many Christian counsellors are too hasty in rushing to moral judgment over the souls who unburden themselves before them, fearing lest they might appear to condone moral lapses or spiritual confusion. They should, like God, be slow to chide and learn to wait for the person to respond to God through conscience and tradition. It does not have to be a matter of giving or with-holding permission for certain types of behaviour. The counsellor does not sit as a magistrate but, in some sense, as a representative and instrument of the Holy Spirit, who guides rather than drags men and women into all truth, including the truth about their own condition. The end to be gained is the enabling of people to take responsibility for their own lives, both for the mistakes they have made and the risks and opportunities that face them. By a patient and generous listening to and engaging with the other person, the counsellor is able to supply that guidance.

The relationship between human counsellors and those they guide is a good analogy of the way we ought to seek that supernatural guidance called Counsel. Again, the central activity is listening, and listening with every part of the personality. It is possible to give this attentiveness to God various technical names, but there is no need to use them at all. Anything that helps us to listen is good, no matter how irregular or eccentric. The most obvious and characteristic method is the almost inescapable practise of silent prayer, the prayer of waiting, of leaning attentively towards God. Many people are able to do this according to the prescribed forms, kneeling upright in church, sitting on a chair at home, in some version of the lotus position, flat on the back on the floor, standing with arms and faces upraised, huddled in a corner wrapped in a cloak. Any of these positions and many I have not mentioned are good listening postures in which we must resist the temptation to fill the emptiness with our own noises, and techniques for dealing with distraction are as legion as postures for prayer. The important principle is gentleness and quietness. We are trying to listen, not impress or overwhelm, so the least effort the better. Fingering beads or a cross can help, so can the occasional repetition of a word or phrase. Some people like to look at an image, others listen to music, others gaze at a lighted candle. But it is a mistake to think that the only way of listening to God, of opening ourselves to his silent in-filling, is by doing something religious or self-consciously prayerful.

It may be that for many the most effective method of opening themselves would be to take long, solitary walks, allowing the mind to drift and ruminate. Some take this a stage further and go on long solitary runs, the regular rhythm of the pace enabling the mind to idle along in a neutral gear. Whatever the chosen technique may be, it should have the effect of disengaging the mind, of enabling it to call off thought awhile so that it might be open to new insights and disclosures. What we are waiting for is something like revelation, some truth or new perspective on truth from beyond the self. Many poems have come to their creators this way, many new scientific discoveries made, many genuine spiritual insights have been received by means of this sort of attentive inattentiveness. What is almost certain is that those who seek the gift of Counsel or divine Guidance must make time for it to happen, and the time must be used in emptying out the distractions and anxiety that clutter our minds and souls. The yogis have taught us that God can fill only the empty cup. We may not ourselves be aware of possessing the gift of Counsel, but others will soon recognize it and use it. And that is just as it should be. None of the gifts of the Holy Spirit is given for our own benefit alone, but by means of them God works to sanctify us and minister to others.

WISDOM and UNDERSTANDING

The novels of Hugh Walpole are probably not read today, but he was once extremely popular and he is the subject of one of the best literary biographies written in the last fifty years. Hugh Walpole was the son of an Anglican priest who ended his career as Bishop of Edinburgh. In his youth it looked very likely that Hugh would follow his father into the ministry, but after graduating from Cambridge he was still undecided. His biographer, Rupert Hart-Davis, makes it clear that Walpole's tussles with vocation were the inevitable result of the impact of his Victorian parents' expectations on his own desires. After Cambridge he agreed to work as a lay missioner with The Missions to Seamen in Liverpool, ostensibly to test his vocation but in reality to postpone it. It was an embarrassing time for him. He lacked the urge to proselytize, found himself tongue-tied about religion. But the Liverpool interlude did decide his vocation. This is how he described the turning-point:

> I went out and down to the Mersey, and there, looking at the river, I had one of the most important hours of my life. That foaming flood tossing in grey froth and

spume out to the sea was invincibly strong and mighty. Ships of all sizes were passing; gulls were wheeling with hoarse screams above my head—the sun broke the clouds and suddenly the river was violet with silver lines and circles.

At that moment I knew. The ferry arrived from the other side; people pushed out and past me. The life and bustle and beauty of the world was everywhere about me. I loved it; I adored it; but not for me to try to change it. Looking out to sea where a great liner slowly took the sun like a queen, I vowed that I would be a novelist, good or bad, for the remainder of my earthly days.

(*Hamish Hamilton Paperback edition, 1985, page 44,* first published by Macmillan, 1952)

The most significant line in that quotation is 'not for me to try to change it'. He tells us that he loved the world, its bustle and its beauty. He did not want to change it. What he dedicated his life to was the description of the world. He would accept it and try to set it down on paper, tell it as he saw it. This is one of the great approaches to writing; the affirmation or celebration of life and the world by reporting it, representing it, and it is captured in the title of Isherwood's most famous book, *I Am A Camera*. Of course, the fascinating implication in Walpole's moment of truth is that it is the function of the priest to change the world. Anyone who accepted life as it comes, apparently, would not be right for the ministry. It is this interventionist or interfering side of Christianity that puts many people off, especially in Britain where people like to be left to themselves. Many people who are attracted to the worship of the Church, who feel real spiritual hunger in themselves, are embarrassed by the evangelistic element in Christianity. People like this do not like being solicited or got at. They feel that spiritual relations should be like sexual relations; voluntary and self-chosen, based on attraction and consent, not on pressure and persuasion. Many people see the evangelist as a sort of spiritual rapist, out to thrust his unsolicited attentions upon unwilling hearers or bent on taking advantage of the lonely and suggestible.

It is difficult not to sympathise with this objection, not to feel a distaste for the avidity with which certain evangelists go into action and work people over. Many Christians must share this sensitivity, for most of them are reluctant to engage in the activity at all, feeling either that they are theologically unequipped for the task of evangelism or too embarrassed to engage in something that seems to require putting pressure on other people to change. There is undoubtedly something decent and attractive in this entirely human reluctance to evangelize. Behind it there often lies, not passivity or cowardice, but a real respect for the freedom of others to live their own lives unmolested by marauding missionaries. This is why the non-evangelistic faiths are so attractive to certain people. Judaism, Catholicism, Orthodoxy, even the Quakers, do their own thing. Any evangelistic pressure is usually of the magnetic sort, and people are drawn to them by their sense of the mystery that is found there and not because they have been grabbed by the shirt collar and made to listen. These great faiths help to mediate the mystery that surrounds us, give us a sense of its glory and attractiveness, but they do not try to compel us to come in. If they sell themselves at all, it is the soft and not the hard sell. They let the world find them; as a rule they don't go after the world.

Of course, this has not always been true of these groups and is not always true today, but it is broadly the case that they do not engage in active proselytizing, unlike other religious groups, Christian and non-Christian. However, Evangelistic groups in the Christian Church have no difficulty in finding support for their activites from both scripture and history. There are many exhortations in the New Testament to make disciples, many injunctions to go out and compel others to come in to the feast, and from the earliest days the Christian movement has been expansionist, going out into all lands to spread the good news. Unlike Hugh Walpole on the banks of the Mersey, it has felt no desire to accept the world as it is, to leave it unchanged. It has felt a compulsion to announce to people the need to change, to turn around and be saved, to become aware of their true condition and the lateness of the hour. Evangelists do not respect the privacy of others or their right to live as they please, because they feel they are in some sort of peril and must be warned about it. They would shout at a man if a tree was about to fall on him or if a car was about to run him down, the danger to him over-riding any right he may have to be undisturbed. Of course, this begs the question about the nature of the human condition and the dangers unreflective human beings face, but if you believe, for instance, that unbaptized pagans go to Hell you will obviously feel it incumbent upon yourself to baptize as many of them as you possibly can. We have not resolved the issue of truth by this recognition, however; we have merely noted that some people like to be left alone, have no desire to change things, while others feel called upon by God to rescue people from perils they unknowingly face, and feel they have a divine licence to interfere in the lives of others. Arriving at absolute truth in this area is probably impossible, but the issue is important as well as interesting, and will bear further examination.

Part of the problem lies with the nature of

zeal. Zeal is not always a good mark for a cause, because it is often a symptom of insecurity and uncertainty, and the zealot's own unadmitted indecisions can lead him to a compensating fanaticism that is often ugly and can be tragic. The Apostle Paul's zealotry against Christianity was almost certainly due, in part, to his own unadmitted doubts about his own cause, and he brought that same embattled and complicated psychological nature into the Christian community, with negative as well as positive results. It is interesting that one of the most zealous figures of the twentieth century wrote one of the most trenchant criticisms of zeal. Bertrand Russell commented on the unlovely zealotry of communists in these words:

> Zeal is a bad mark for a cause. Nobody has any zeal about arithmetic. It is not the vaccinationists but the anti-vaccinationists who generate zeal. People are zealous for a cause when they are not quite positive that it is true.

Of course, zeal is often less sinister than that. It can be the mark of ardent personalities who throw themselves into all their affairs with relentless enthusiasm. This kind of zeal can be disarming and infectious, or it can be merely boring, but it tells us more about the personality of the zealot than it does about the cause he is currently espousing. If zealotry is suspect, therefore, and likely either to offend people or overpersuade them, then straightforward advocacy is likely to win a hearing even if it does not gain agreement. Advocates need not be zealots, but they do need a cause, they must have a brief, something to plead. In fact, they are out to change people's minds about something, so Hugh Walpole was half right in his perception, although I suspect that he was reacting against a certain type of evangelism and not the thing in itself. After all, we can do the right thing for the wrong reason, and even if we try to do the right thing for the right reason we can do it badly. Finding the balance between a proper advocacy of Christian truth and a respect for the rights and freedom of others to reject or differ from that truth is difficult, but it is the gift of the wise and understanding evangelist. The gift of understanding, of a true appreciation of the situation and all its circumstances, is a rare and precious gift, worth struggling to receive.

At the beginning of the search for understanding must come self-knowledge. The understanding pastor and preacher, like the understanding friend, must know himself and his own inadequacies and vulnerabilities, both personally and theologically. Reinhold Niebuhr recognized this very well; he knew the swamps of selfrighteousness into which the unwary preacher could fall:

Whenever a prophet is born, either inside or outside of the church, he faces the problem of preaching repentance without bitterness and of criticizing without spiritual pride. . . . Think of sitting Sunday after Sunday under some professional holy man who is constantly asserting his egotism by criticizing yours. I would rebel, if I were a layman. A spiritual leader who has too many illusions is useless. One who has lost his illusions about mankind and retains his illusions about himself is insufferable. Let the process of disillusionment continue until the self is included. At that point, of course, only religion can save from the enervation of despair. But it is at that point that true religion is born.

(*Leaves from the Notebook of a Tamed Cynic*)

The only valid evangelism is humble evangelism, the invitation to share in a pilgrimage, to embark on a process of exploration, to begin to know a mysterious stranger; it is not the handing down of a complete assembly kit for the construction of an instant salvation machine. At the heart of the Christian attempt to change the world is the knowledge that something is amiss, that there is a profound distortion at the heart of things, including the lives of ordinary people, that needs to be worked against. Christianity is a religion of redemption, it believes that men and women need to be saved from that side of their nature that pulls them destructively into themselves. The shorthand word for that tendency is sin, but it is a complex phenomenon and is not patient of simple solutions, though many are on offer. We could enlarge on the nature of sin in many ways. For instance, our own century affords countless examples of the hideous effects of collective evil, the most clearly documented example being the six million Jews killed by Hitler, but there are other examples about which less is known, though the statistics are even more horrifying. It is estimated that Stalin was responsible for the deaths of ten million kulaks, and the deaths imposed by Mao during the Great Leap Forward are said to be in the region of twenty-seven million. The assassinations in Cambodia, per head of population, are said to be the highest of the century, and the purges and pogroms in African states during the last thirty years probably run well into the millions.

So Walpole's idyll on the banks of the Mersey is not the only perspective on the world. Given the dimensions of the human tragedy, it is not surprising that the voices of prophets and evangelists have been in unceasing cry against the crimes and follies of mankind. Most of us in the nations of the North West are personally unacquainted with such depths of evil, though our television screens make us all-too aware of them in other places. But even in our own unremarkable lives we are aware of struggles and distortions, keenly aware of the many ways in which we trap ourselves in our selfishness and trip ourselves up by our own weaknesses. Any life, even if it is unvisited by great tragedy or kept free from involvement in great horrors, is a struggle towards balance and wisdom. Most of us know something of struggle and the longing for change: the struggle to be faithful and ordinarily kind; the struggle against destructive habits, even the struggle to keep our weight down, so commonplace in our overfed society. Tiny conflicts, perhaps, but ways in which the phenomenon of sin focusses itself in our own unremarkable lives. And this need not be a heavily tragic awareness. There can be humour in it, a certain wistfulness, a wry awareness that our problems may not be cosmic but that they do occupy much of our energy. This unspectacular awareness of what we are like need not be obsessional, but it should be truthful. It should keep us quietly humble, and more understanding of the follies of others. We should carry it with us always, not as a voice constantly shouting in our ears, but as a whisper that is always just under the surface. We are flawed. One of the gentlest and most winning examples of this spirit is found in John Betjeman's poem *A Lincolnshire Church*. He comes across this church in the Lincolnshire wold, apparently unregarded and uncared for:

> And around it, turning their backs,
> The usual sprinkle of villas;
> The usual woman in slacks,
> Cigarette in her mouth,
> Regretting Americans, stands
> As a wireless croons in the kitchen
> Manicuring her hands.
> Dear old, bloody old England
> Of telegraph poles and tin,
> Seemingly so indifferent
> And with so little soul to win.

He enters.

> The great door shuts, and lessens
> That roar of churchyard trees
> And the Presence of God Incarnate
> Has brought me to my knees.
> 'I acknowledge my transgressions'
> The well-known phrases rolled
> With thunder sailing over
> From the heavily clouded wold.
> 'And my sin is ever before me'.

Just that. No overwhelming dramatics. My sin is ever before me, that's all.

That is the spirit Niebuhr was pleading for, and it is essential in the Christian who is seeking to commend the Faith. It rescues us from unlovely zealotry, from dishonest advocacy. If the fear of God is the beginning of wisdom, then self-knowledge is the beginning of understanding. And an aspect of that self-knowledge pertains to our Faith. There should be humility here as well. We never entirely possess faith and we are never entirely true to it. We are always to some extent unworthy servants, bearers of tidings whose import we obscure by our own egotism. That is why, like St Paul, we should not be afraid to expose our weaknesses, even in belief. One of Unamuno's great declarations sums it up perfectly:

> Those who believe they believe in God, but without passion in their heart, without anguish of mind, without uncertainty, without doubt and even at times without despair, believe only in the idea of God, not in God himself.

But the quest for understanding should not end with candid self-knowledge, the admission of our frailty; it should extend to the mysteries of our Faith, too. Most of us are selective about the Faith, taking the bits that appeal to some aspect of our nature or personality. Pessimists stress the reality of sin and optimists celebrate the promise of hope. And here I want to come back to Hugh Walpole on the banks of the Mersey. He was on to something valid and something that is found in the Christian tradition. Christianity is a religion of redemption, it holds out the possibility of transformation; but it is also a religion of affirmation, it wants us to learn to see the world aright, to detect the glory of God in the midst of things as they are. The great theological doctrines that enclose this insight are the Creation and the Incarnation, the doctrine that the creation is good and that God has entered it and is to be encountered through it.

Fully to understand these doctrines is to be liberated from certain kinds of depression and despair. We do not have to import God into the situation; he is already there and we have only to discern the signs of his presence. And those signs are found in ordinary human kindness and cheerfulness, as well as in extraordinary human heroism and self-sacrifice. Christians are not always to be chiding the world, scolding and berating it; sometimes they are to celebrate it, be its instrument of praise. One of the vexing things about Christian history is the way the doctrine of redemption becomes separated from the doctrines of Creation and Incarnation, leading to strangely truncated institutions that proclaim only part of the Faith and end by either accepting everything or accepting nothing. Understanding Christians will recognize that the world is flawed, but they will know that it is an ungenerous and ungracious mind that sees only flaws in God's creation. The understanding mind, like the gentle author of Psalm 103, will know whereof we are made, remembering that we are but dust; but it will also recognize that

God has destined that dust for glory, and that it reflects the glory even now.

The gift of understanding is the gift of balance, a true awareness of the situation. It knows when to affirm and when to deny, when to celebrate and when to lament. And neither in its sorrowing nor in its rejoicing is it overbearing, proud or rude. The gift of understanding is an inescapable element in the commendation of the Christian Faith to a world that has so often perceived Christians to be harsh and censorious, self-deluded and cocksure. It must not be mistaken for weakness, though it usually issues in gentleness. After all, it is only the truly strong who know how to be truly gentle.

The gift of understanding is the prelude to Wisdom itself, which is the cumulative result of all the gifts in operation. The wise person is the whole, the rounded person, displaying all the characteristic endowments of the Holy Spirit, expressing harmoniously the effect of the sevenfold gift. And the gift of holy fear is the beginning of this cumulative endowment. Fear is truly the beginning of wisdom, because it establishes a true proportion between the self and God. We are not, of course, talking about craven or pathological fear, but of that true fear that establishes proportions and recognizes consequences. The presence of this sort of disposition leads to a realistic, rueful, almost humorous awareness of our true state as utterly dependent upon

God, yet strangely in struggle against him. The closer we draw to God the more awe we feel, yet we experience a strange combination of dread and acceptance. God's dreadful majesty is experienced as being conterminous with his mercy, and recognition of this duality means that fear is succeeded by or is co-active with that grateful reverence we call piety. Piety is our patrial love, the feeling we have for the one to whom we belong, whose mercy is as his majesty.

The experience of both fear and piety, dread and affectionate reverence, rescues us from a false and truncated knowledge of God, leading either to guilt and repression or a spoiled indifference and familiarity. Our knowledge of God is as true to his nature as we can make it, leading to a state of balance and harmony that supplies us with the courage or fortitude we need for a life of steady and purposive discipleship. The gifts of counsel and understanding are the most subtle of the six elements that create the wise and rounded character. Under the guidance of the Spirit the soul is led to a type of surrender and self-effacement that allows a genuine openness towards others on the one hand, and a radical self-awareness on the other. These are the gifts that put the self in proportion, leading to a healthy sort of humility that places a proper restraint upon the intrusive egotism that distorts all our human relationships. Finally, when fear, piety, knowledge, courage, counsel and under-standing are all at work within us, balancing and modifying each other, the result is the creation of holy wisdom, the crown of all the gifts.